Bright Gem of the Western Seas

DATE			

(MAP fold. in back of
Book) — missing

© THE BAKER & TAYLOR CO.

Bright Gem
of the
Western Seas

CALIFORNIA 1846-1852

Early Recollections of the Mines
Tulare Plains
Life in California
by James H. Carson

A Report of the Tulare Valley
by Lieutenant George H. Derby

Edited by Peter Browning

GREAT WEST BOOKS   LAFAYETTE, CALIFORNIA

Cover design by Larry Van Dyke and Peter Browning
Cover engraving of Fort Point and the Golden Gate
    from John Russell Bartlett's
    Personal Narrative . . . during the years 1850, '51, '52, and '53

Printed in the United States of America

Great West Books
PO Box 1028
Lafayette, CA 94549

Library of Congress Cataloging-in-Publication Data

Bright gem of the western seas : California, 1846–1852 / edited by
    Peter Browning.
        p.   cm.
    Includes index.
    Contents: Early recollections of the mines. Tulare plains. Life in
    California / by James H. Carson — A report of the Tulare valley /
    by George H. Derby.
    ISBN 0-944220-05-3 (pbk. : alk. paper).
    1. California—Description and travel—1848–1869.
    2. California—Gold discoveries.
    3. California—History—1846–1850.
    4. San Joaquin River Valley (Calif.)—Description and travel.
    I. Browning, Peter, 1928–   . II. Carson, James H., d. 1853.
    III. Derby, George Horatio, 1823–1861.
    F865.B846   1991
    979.4'04—dc20   91–4032
                                                              CIP

Contents

Early Recollections of the Mines

Tulare Plains

Life in California

A report of the Tulare Valley

Index

Illustrations

Editor's Preface

It is my belief that there is no finer and more accurate way to present basic history than to use the words of those who made the history—who observed and participated in the events of their day, and had the ability to record those events and their impressions of their times in lucid, vibrant language.

When I first came across James H. Carson's articles—in the course of many hours spent reading old newspapers on microfilm—I was so struck by their content and by Carson's extensive use of the peculiarly Californian idiom of the 1850s that I was certain I wanted to publish them as a book. I soon learned that they had been done in book form three times, but in an altered sequence and never in their entirety. In effect, no one but the newspaper's readers in early 1852 had ever seen all that Carson wrote.

The report by Lieutenant George H. Derby of his reconnaissance of the Tulare (San Joaquin) Valley in the spring of 1850 was a perfect match with Carson's articles. Derby's report—as well as his report of his 1849 reconnaissance of the Sacramento Valley in 1849—was reprinted, with an introduction and notes by Francis P. Farquhar, in the *California Historical Society Quarterly* in 1932. But that is nearly six decades ago, and although the reports are sometimes cited by historians, they are essentially unknown to today's readers.

Neither Derby's report nor Carson's articles nor the three editions of the book made from the articles contained illustrations. Since I thought it necessary to illustrate this book, I had perforce to acquire illustrations from whatever sources came to mind—or to hand. I had a few potential items in my possession, but most of what I have used comes from the collections at the Bancroft Library in Berkeley and the California State Library in Sacramento. Those illustrations that were taken from other books of the period have the author's last name and the title of the book following their captions.

The list below provides more complete information on these books, including dates of first publication.

Bartlett, John Russell. *Personal Narrative . . . during the Years 1850, '51, '52, and '53.* New York & London: D. Appleton & Company, 1854. The source for the cover illustration.

Borthwick, John David. *Three Years in California.* Edinburgh & London: Wm. Blackwood & sons, 1857. Reprinted in 1948 by Biobooks, Oakland.

Colton, Walter. *Three Years in California.* [1846–1849]. New York: Barnes; and Cincinnati: H. W. Derby & Co., 1850. Reprinted in 1948 by Biobooks, Oakland; and by Stanford University Press, 1949.

Delano, Alonzo. *Old Block's Sketch Book,* illustrated by Charles Nahl. Sacramento: James Anthony & Co., 1856. Reprinted in 1947 by Fine Arts Press, Santa Ana.

Gerstäcker, Friedrich Wilhelm Christian. *Scènes de la vie Californienne.* Genève: Imprimerie de Jules-Gme. Fick, 1859. Reprinted in 1942 in English, as *Scenes of Life in California,* by J. Howell, San Francisco.

Marryat, Francis Samuel. *Mountains and Molehills, or, Recollections of a Burnt Journal.* New York: Harper, 1855. Reprinted in 1952 by Stanford University Press.

Revere, Joseph Warren. *A Tour of Duty in California.* New York: C. S. Francis & Co.; and Boston: J. H. Francis, 1849. Reprinted in 1947 by Biobooks, Oakland, with the title of *Naval Duty in California.*

Soulé, Frank; Gihon, John H.; and Nisbet, James. *The Annals of San Francisco.* New York: D. Appleton & Company; San Francisco: Montgomery Street; London: 16 Little Britain, 1855. Reprinted in 1966 by L. Osborne, Palo Alto.

Vischer, Edward. *Vischer's Pictorial of California.* San Francisco: J. Winterburn & Co., 1870.

On several occasions, in footnotes, I cite Sherburne (S. F.) Cook, who wrote extensively from the 1940s to the 1970s on California Indians and on Spanish expeditions into the San Joaquin Valley between 1800 and 1840. I also make brief references to the 1776 journey of Father Francisco Garcés. His diary was first published in English as *On the Trail of a Spanish Pioneer*, translated and edited by Elliott Coues. (New York: Harper, 1900.) A new translation, by John Galvin, was published as *A Record of Travels in Arizona and California, 1775–1776*. (San Francisco: John Howell—Books, 1965.)

Carson, or perhaps the typesetter for the newspaper, engaged in some unusual punctuation, especially in the first series of articles. The 1852 book corrected most of these inadequacies and confusions. I have changed the punctuation in several places—whenever it seemed that the meaning of a given passage had been altered by a misplaced comma or semicolon. In fewer than ten instances I have corrected the spelling of a word when it was obvious that the mis-spelling was a typographic error rather than a quaint or archaic usage. Other than these limited, minor alterations, the text is exactly as it appeared in Carson's 1852 newspaper articles and in Derby's report. I have retained punctuation that is not correct by present standards, and have also retained several typographic conventions of that day that are now done differently. These are: a semicolon preceding a closing quotation mark rather than following it; a comma preceding a closing parenthesis rather than following it; and a comma immediately before an em dash rather than just the dash alone.

Carson frequently created sentences with a plural subject and a singular verb, or vice versa, and occasionally used the wrong verb tense. Once in a while he stumbled into such awkward syntax that one has to read a passage twice to understand what he meant. I have retained all of these errors, and have refrained from introducing [*sic*] every time one of them appears. Except for the spelling corrections noted in the preceding paragraph, I have also retained the spellings of both Carson and Derby, even when they spelled the same word in different ways. Any word or words in brackets are my additions or are explained in a footnote.

Editor's Introduction

James H. Carson

James H. Carson, a native of Virginia and the author of the first three parts of this book, arrived in California in January 1847. He was Second Sergeant in Company F, 3rd Artillery, of the regular army. The regiment embarked at New York on the U.S. ship *Lexington* on July 14, 1846. En route to California the vessel touched at Rio de Janeiro, doubled Cape Horn in October, called at Valparaiso in November, and anchored at Monterey on January 28, 1847. By this time the conquest of California was complete, and Company F settled down to garrison duty in Monterey.

Gold was discovered at Coloma on January 24, 1848. The discovery had the same affect on Company F that it had on thousands of people across the country and around the world: many dropped what they were doing and headed for the diggings. By the end of August the company had lost thirty-three men to desertion, and only about fifty men were still on duty. As he recounts, Carson resisted the temptation for a while, but then—apparently on a furlough—

> He was seized with this new western dance of St. Vitus, and was carried on an old mule to the gold-diggings. He began work at Mormon Island by annihilating earth in his wash-basin, standing up to his knees in water, slashing and splashing as if resolving the universe to its original elements. Fifty pans of dirt thus pulverized gave the fevered pilgrim but fifty cents; whereupon a deep disgust filled his soul, and immediately with the departure of his malady the man departed. On passing through Weber's Indian trading camp, however, he saw such heaps of glittering gold as brought the ague on again more violent than ever, resulting in a prolonged stay at Kelsey's and Hangtown. (Bancroft, *History of California*, vol. vi, 96–97.)

In August 1848 Carson joined a party of miners that began to prospect farther south. They worked all the streams down to the Stanislaus River, and there parted company. Carson made a good strike, claiming that he and several others each took out 180 ounces of gold in ten days; Carson Creek and the hamlet of Carson Hill were named for him. Heavy rains came in October, and drove the miners out to the cities,

In the spring of 1849 Carson helped to organize the Carson-Robinson party of ninety-two men for the purpose of prospecting in unexplored areas. They crossed the San Joaquin Valley and reached the Sierra foothills at about Mariposa Creek, and from there prospected northward until they arrived again at Carson Creek and Angels Creek.

In 1850 Carson and a Dr. Roberts formed a partnership to establish a trading business between Stockton and Mariposa. It apparently never came to anything, since Carson came down with a severe attack of rheumatism and became an invalid. He was hospitalized for eighteen months, and after that time went to Stockton to recuperate. A Stockton newspaper, *The San Joaquin Republican*, announced his arrival in the issue of January 14, 1852.

> Mr. James H. Carson, a pioneer in California, and the discoverer of the celebrated Carson's Creek, has arrived in town. He is on his way to the scene of his early discoveries; we are sorry to say that he has been an invalid for the past 18 months, in the Monterey Hospital, and has lost the use of his speech. He has kindly consented to furnish the readers of the *Republican* with various interesting particulars in reference to the early history of the Gold Diggings.

Between January 17 and May 29 the newspaper printed the thirty-three articles, in three series, that are contained in this book. The first two series, "Early Recollections of the Mines" and "Tulare Plains," were published in a separate form in late March, "at a low price, done up in neat wrappers, for transmission by the post." In June the *Republican* added the "Life in California" series, and reissued the whole as a book—the first book ever published in Stockton. It has been republished twice since then, in 1931 and 1950.

Nowhere in these three editions does one learn that a significant portion of the original material was omitted. I estimate that about thirty percent of it has not been printed since it was in the 1852 newspapers. Much of the rest was rearranged when it was put into book form, in such a manner that the continuity of the articles was sometimes lost. The two reprint editions simply replicated the 1852 book; there is no indication that the publishers of those reprints knew that something was missing.

The *Republican* was proud of what Carson had produced, and I cannot do better than to quote the editors of that paper in the issue of May 22, 1852 as they ballyhooed the forthcoming book.

> Our readers must have perused these life-like pictures of scenes and characters in California, and admired them as the true reflex of affairs here, both in the early days of the gold fever, and of things as they are in the present somewhat more sober days. There is an *abandon* in the style, a peculiar choice of language, a broad humor, and a liberal soul about them, which are characteristics peculiarly Californian. It is impossible to transfer to paper the characters of scenes here, in the sober language of the *Belles Lettres* of the Eastern world—any more than you can render in plain Anglo Saxon the *coversazione* of Paris. Our scenes, to be truly presented, must appear in our language, and in our own loose and *fast* spirit. Mr. Carson has mixed with all classes of persons in this country—was guide to Gov. Mason and Gen. Riley in their expeditions to the mines, of which we have all heard so much—adventured himself into the first blaze of the gold excitement; discovered Carson's Creek; made gold there by the *hundred* weight; but, having a lively imagination, afterwards lost it all; got his constitution out of repair, and has anchored at the State Hospital in this city, where he has been obliging us and amusing himself with writing a history of his travels and adventures.

Later in 1852 the Whigs of Calaveras County desired to nominate Carson to run for the legislature, but he declined. In the spring of 1853 he ran for the state assembly on the Democratic ticket, and was elected by a large majority. Before he could take office he had another serious attack of rheumatism, and died in Stockton about April 20. His widow and daughter arrived in California a month later, nearly destitute. A collection was made on their behalf, and they returned to the East.

Carson was a product of his time. One could make a case that what he said was new, original, visionary—but this is true only in the sense that he was the first of the early miners to pen a "I Recollect" memoir. His series on the Tulare Valley (now the San Joaquin Valley) is indeed original, but his prescriptions of what to do with this unproductive, semi-arid region were driven by the predominant American idea of the mid-nineteenth century: Manifest Destiny. If ever there was a Manifest Destiny man, Carson is the paradigm. He believed that it was the fate of the United States to conquer and settle the continent; to make the land to bud and "blossom as the rose"; to overwhelm the animal-like natives who stood in the way; to exploit *everything* there is that could possibly be exploited—the minerals, the animals, the soil, the water, everything—all must succumb to the righteous, conquering spirit. Carson's thoughts on damming rivers and irrigating the barren lands sound prophetic: those are indeed the things that have come to pass, but on a gargantuan scale that Carson could not have imagined and with dire results that no one expected.

Carson anticipated the railroad, knowing for a certainty that it would come and being wrong only in predicting its most likely route. He looked beyond the end of the continent, and prophesied that America's—or California's—destiny lay in the Pacific. Perhaps the American flag someday would wave over the Hawaiian or Japanese islands.

Carson also had the attitudes—common at the time—of one whom we would undoubtedly now castigate as a racist. His contempt for and hatred of Indians was pure and naked. (Two and three-fourths of the articles in the "Tulare Plains" series are about Indians; they were not included in the 1852 book.)

But the purpose of printing James Carson's articles in their entirety is neither to condemn nor to praise. It is to present to the people of the present time a better notion of what it was to be one of the early miners, an explorer of California lands as yet uninhabited by Americans, and one who remembered—in perhaps a superficial and romantic way—the lives of the Mexican/Californians just before California was conquered and the immigrants rushed in.

George Horatio Derby

George Horatio Derby (1823–1861), born in Dedham, Massachusetts, graduated from West Point in 1846 and was assigned to the
topographical engineers. His first duty was to survey the harbor of
New Bedford, Massachusetts. During the Mexican War he saw action
at Cerro Gordo, where he was wounded. After the war Derby explored and surveyed in Minnesota, and then spent a year at the
Topographical Bureau in Washington, where he polished his skills as
a topographical draftsman. He then was transferred to the Far West,
arriving at Monterey by ship on June 10, 1849. During the next two
years he led four field expeditions for the purposes of exploration,
road-building, and mapping.

The first of these expeditions was a reconnaissance of a portion of
the San Joaquin and Sacramento valleys in September 1849. Derby's
report, with an excellent accompanying map, was printed in House
of Representatives Executive Document No. 17, 31st Congress, 1st
Session, 1850. Derby spent the winter of 1849–50 in Monterey, and
in April and May of 1850 made the reconnaissance of the "Tulare
Valley," as the lower part of the San Joaquin Valley was then called.
His report was not published for another two years: Senate Executive Document No. 110, 32d Congress, 1st Session, 1852. Derby's
superbly done map, which accompanied the report, was far superior
to anything that existed up to that time. It has been reproduced at
full size from an original copy. Although the gold discovery had occurred more than two years earlier, there were as yet no towns in
the Central Valley south of the San Joaquin River. Indeed, the only
whites encountered by Derby south of the San Joaquin were three
men who were operating two ferries across the Kings River, and a
man by himself on his way to establish a ferry across the Kern.

Derby's report is lucid and detailed, and is replete with precise
descriptions of Indians and the terrain—especially of the appearance
and scope of Tulare Lake and Buena Vista Lake, which have long
since vanished. (It should be noted that when Derby referred to the
head or upper end of the Tulare Valley, he meant the south end.)
Derby was a skilled engineer and cartographer, a man who took his
military duties seriously, and in fact comes across as the diametric
opposite of his other persona: *alias* Squibob, *alias* John Phœnix.

Derby's renown is as California's first humorist—a wit and a wag of great imagination and originality, a legendary practical joker, a satirist, and a drawer of absurd illustrations. He used his talents to puncture the pompous and to lampoon staid conventions.

His articles appeared originally in California newspapers and periodicals. A collection of these articles was published in 1856 as *Phœnixiana*; it eventually went to twenty-six printings. Another collection, the *Squibob Papers*, was published in 1865. George R. Stewart wrote a biography of Derby: *John Phoenix, Esq., The Veritable Squibob* (1937). And in 1990 Richard Derby Reynolds, a distant relative of George Horatio Derby, resurrected the best of Derby's articles under the title of *Squibob, An Early California Humorist*.

Lieutenant Derby conducted a four-month-long expedition to the Gulf of California and the lower Colorado River during the winter of 1850–51. Later he went back east, but returned to California in November 1852 and was stationed at San Diego for two years. He was married at San Francisco in January 1854. He then spent a year in the Oregon Territory, returned to San Francisco, and sailed for Panama and the East in November 1856. During the remainder of his military career he was engaged in constructing lighthouses at various places on the coast of the Gulf of Mexico. He apparently suffered sunstroke—or some other debilitating illness—and was on sick leave for the last year and a half of his life. He died in May 1861 at the age of thirty-eight, leaving a wife and three children.

PETER BROWNING

Early Recollections of the Mines

The Gold Fever

HAVING SEEN MANY COMMUNICATIONS in the various papers printed in California, on different subjects of interest to the people, I am prompted to furnish a few particulars connected with the history of the times and people in California, from 1846 to '52.

The military and naval operations, the conquest and acquirement of California, are matters of history, and are now before the people.

To the "good old times" now past, when each day was big with the wonders and discoveries of rich diggings, I would like to principally confine my observations.

A party of Mormons, who were constructing a saw mill, (where Coloma now stands,) under Mr. Marshall, it is well known, first discovered that gold was to be had here for the trouble of picking it up. After they had procured a small quantity of the dust, they hastened to that old knight of pioneers, Capt. Sutter, for consultation. What the shining scales were they could not properly decide, but they thought it was gold; it looked like it, felt like it, and the STUFF had no suspicious "*smell!*"

San Francisco, which then consisted of seven or eight houses, scattered along the sand hills, was consulted, and the *metal pronounced to be virgin gold.* The effect that this decision had on our quiet citizens was electric. The population of California, at that day, consisted of hardy, brave, and quiet men, who had travelled over the trackless wilderness, with their wives and little ones, their flocks and herds; and amidst dangers, toils, and sufferings, had reached the western confines of our continent, and unfurled the broad banner of freedom, and beneath it were quietly cultivating our rich valleys, unconscious of the gold laden hills that surrounded them. The first reports of the immense quantities of gold found in every river, gulch, and ravine, was not believed by these good pioneers of 1846, but the continued arrival of pounds, *arobas*, and *fanegas* of the precious metal,[1] soon quieted all doubts on the subject, and a general stampede took place in the different settlements. The many comic scenes that were enacted would fill a volume of humor. Men who, ere then, were content to labor years for a few hundred dollars, and many hard-working honest fellows who never had twenty dollars at one time in their lives, were now fully convinced that they had but to procure a pick, pan, and knife, go to the gold region, and their *eternal fortins* were made. I was at that time (1848) a resident of the then flourishing City of Monterey. The months of April and May had carried off many of our inhabitants—not to their long homes, but to the gold mines. Many of the old fellows who had put the whole golden reports down as "dod drat" humbug, had one after another gone to the mines. Some had left privately to prevent the remainder from laughing at them, while others, bordering on insanity, raved around crying for pickaxe, shovel, and pan, [and] had started off at railroad speed. The month of May, with all her flowers and balmy air had approached, and I an unbeliever still. One day I saw a form, bent and filthy, approaching me, and soon a cry of recognition was given between us. He was an old acquaintance, and had gone amongst the first to the mines. Now he stood before me:

> "His hair hung out of his hat,
> His chin with beard was black,
> And his buckskins reached but to his knees;
> An old flannel shirt he wore,
> Which many a bush had tore:"

---

1. An aroba is a Spanish unit of weight of between 25 and 36 pounds; a fanega is a bulk measure, about a bushel and a half. Carson is simply saying that gold was arriving in huge quantities.

Yes, Billy, I can see you yet, just as you stood before me on that sunny 10th of May, looking so much like the devil, with that great bag of the Tempter on your back! Then he told me it was gold, and that he had made it in five weeks in Kelsey's[2] and the dry diggings (where Hangtown now is).[3] I could not believe it, but told him that the proof would be in his bag, which was soon opened, and out the metal tumbled; not in dust or scales, but in pieces ranging in size from that of a pea to hen's eggs; and, says he, "this is only what I picked out with a knife." There was before me proof positive that I had held too long to the wrong side of the question. I looked on for a moment; a frenzy seized my soul; unbidden my legs performed some entirely new movements of Polka steps—I took several—houses were too small for me to stay in; I was soon in the street in search of the necessary outfits; piles of gold rose up before me at every step; castles of marble, dazzling the eye with their rich appliances; thousands of slaves, bowing to my beck and call; myriads of fair virgins contending with each other for my love, were among the fancies of my fevered imagination. The Rothschilds, Girard and Astors appeared to me but poor people; in short, I had a very violent attack of the *Gold Fever.*

One hour after I became thus affected, I was mounted on an old mule, armed with a wash hand basin, fire shovel, a piece of square iron pointed at one end, a blanket, a rifle, a few yards of jerked beef, and a bag of *penola,* and going at high pressure mule speed for the diggin's.

No roads marked the way to the traveller in California then; but, guided by the sun and well known mountain peaks, we proceeded on our journey. No ferries were in operation for our passage across the deep and rapid streams. The site of your now beautiful and flourishing city of Stockton, was then alone in its native greatness; no steamboat's whistle was heard to startle the affrighted elk; nor had the newsboys' call been heard, or solemn bell called forth the sons of prayer. But still there was a little *mud.* Heedless of all difficulties, on, on I sped, until Mormon Island, on the South Fork,[4] brought me

---

2. Named for Benjamin Kelsey; gold was found here in 1848. The site is on the road between Placerville and Georgetown.
3. Gold was discovered at Dry Diggings in April 1848; the town that arose there was nicknamed Hangtown. It was named Placerville in 1850.
4. Gold was discovered at this site on the South Fork of the American River in March 1848 by two Mormons. The location is now under Folsom Lake.

up. Some forty or fifty men were at work with the cradle machines, and were averaging about 8 oz. per day to the man. But a few moments passed before I was knee deep in water with my wash basin full of dirt, plunging it about, trying to separate the dirt from the gold. After washing some fifty pans of dirt, I found I had realised about four bits worth of gold. Reader, do you know how an *hombre* feels when the gold fever has suddenly fallen to about zero? I do. Kelsey's and the old dry diggings had just been opened, and to them I next set out; a few hours ride brought me to the Indian trading camp of Capt. Weber's famed company, where I saw sights of gold that revived the *fever* again. I saw Indians giving handfuls of gold for a cotton handkerchief or a shirt; and so great was the income of the Captain's trading houses that he was daily sending out mules packed with gold, to the settlements. And no man in California was more deserving of this good fortune than Capt. Weber; he was one of the men of the Bear Flag.[5] His time and fortunes had been given to the American cause, and he was ever seen in our ranks where danger threatened. Geology had not been deeply studied by our sons of the "forest wild," and many were the conjectures formed *whar* the gold came from; they could find it in the river anywhere; and at last they came to the sage conclusion that it was washed down from some place where the earth was a bed of gold, and as it continued to tumble about, became worn into the thin scales as they found it. As I have intimated, to find the source from whence the gold came was the great object, and many prospecting parties were soon out with this purpose in view. The Indians who were working for Captains Sutter and Weber gave them leading information, so that they were enabled to know the direction in which new discoveries were to be made.

A party accompanied Mr. Kelsey and discovered the first dry diggings, which were named Kelsey's diggings, after their discoverer. The next discovered was the old dry diggings, out of which so many thousands of dollars have since been taken. Amongst the pioneers

---

5. Charles M. Weber, a native of Germany, came to California in 1841 with the Bartleson-Bidwell party, the first emigrant wagon train to reach California. He founded the town of Tuleburg, which he renamed Stockton in honor of Commodore Robert F. Stockton, who had taken possession of California for the United States.

of these discoveries were Dr. Isabell, Daniel and John Murphy, (who were connected with Capt. Weber's trading establishments,) Messrs. Murray and Phalen, of San Jose; Messrs. Kensey and Aram, of Monterey.[6] The old dry diggings were situated at Hangtown, in El Dorado county. In June, July, and August, 1848, it was the centre of attraction for gold diggers. The population then there, (exclusive of Indians,) consisted of about three hundred,—old pioneers, native Californians, deserters from the Army, Navy, and Colonel Stevenson's volunteers, were there mingled together, the happiest set of men the mind can conjure up. Every man had plenty of *dust*. From three ounces, to five pounds, was the income per day to him *who would work*. The gulches and ravines were opened about two feet wide and one foot in depth along their centres, and the gold picked out from amongst the dirt with a knife. When they failed to realise two or three ounces per day by this method, the diggings were pronounced *worked out*, and new ones were hunted up.

Clothing was not to be had for love or gold; and I have seen many an *hombre* with as much gold as he could carry, whose skin

"Peeped out through many a rent."

The miner's bill of fare consisted of beef, bread, sugar, and coffee, at from two to four dollars per pound—and scarce at that; varied at times with a box of sardines, at $20 per box. Amongst our population of that golden day, we had *one* Jew. The old miners will ever remember Dutch John. When I arrived in the diggings, old friends hailed from every side, and an invitation was soon given all hands to go down to Dutch John's and take a *big drink*. As John's store was about a fair sample of the trading establishments of the day, a short description may not be uninteresting:

The *building*, like all others then used, consisted of brush cut from the neighboring trees; his stock of goods: two boxes of crackers, a few boxes of sardines, a few knives, (samples of every pattern ever made,) a half box of tobacco, and two barrels of the *youngest* whiskey I had ever tasted. The counter was the head of an empty barrel, set off with a broken tumbler, tin cup, and a junk bottle of the ardent.

---

6. All of these were early emigrants or were with the various military contingents engaged in the conquest of California. Daniel and John Murphy are the namesakes of the town of Murphys.

Scales and weights were not then much in use, and John's store had
none. A drink was paid for by his taking a *pinch* of gold dust with his
thumb and fore-finger from the miner's bag! or, sorting out a lump
the size or value of a dollar, according to Jewish ideas of such things.
Before taking the pinch from the bag, John's finger and thumb could
be seen sliding down his throat (as far as the balance of the hand
would permit) for the purpose of covering them with saliva, to make
the gold stick, and he then thrust it into the miners *pile*. The amount
of such a pinch was from four to eight dollars! *"Got und Himmel!"*
John—if we have accounts to settle in the next world, won't the
clerks have a time of it with yours! This mode of settling was taken
rather as a source of fun for the miners than an imposition.

A United States deserter, from the fort at Monterey, on his way to the mines, upon the
back of a mule, which the Vulture claims. (Colton, *Three Years in California*.)

The Northern Mines in 1848

THE FIRST SCALES FOR WEIGHING GOLD were made by taking a piece of pine wood for the beam, pieces of sardine boxes for scales, and silver dollars for weights. Gold dust could be purchased in any quantities at four and five dollars per ounce in the diggings, and for six and eight dollars in the coast towns.

Sutter's Fort was the great mart for trade. Sutter's Embarcadero, where the city of Sacramento now is, was the landing place for goods from San Francisco, from which place they were transported to the stores at the fort, and there exposed for sale.

Honesty, (which we now have so little of,) was the ruling passion amongst the miners of '48. Old debts were paid up; heavy bags of gold dust were carelessly left laying in their brush houses; mining tools, though scarce, were left in their places of work for days at a time, and not one theft or robbery was committed.

Sutter's Fort in 1848. (J. W. Revere, *A Tour of Duty in California*.)

In August, the old diggings were pronounced as being "dug out," and many prospecting parties had gone out. Part of Weber's trading establishments had secretly disappeared, and rumors were afloat that the place where all the gold "came from" had been discovered South, and a general rush of the miners set that way.

Before bidding farewell to the Northern mines, and taking the reader South—I would remark, that the South and North fork of the American river, Feather and Yuba rivers, Kelsey's and the old Dry Diggings, were all that had been worked at this date. The Middle and North fork were discovered by a few deserters, in September, where in the space of a few days they realised from five to twenty thousand dollars each, and they left California by the first conveyance. Tools for mining purposes were scarce and high; a pick, pan and shovel ranging from $50 to $200; butchers knives from $10 to $25; and cradle washing machines from $200 to $800 each. Provisions were worth $2 per pound; woolen shirts $50 each; boots and shoes from $25 to $150 pair.

The discovery of Sutter's Creek[1] and Rio Seco[2] was made in July, and the Moquelumne river diggings, at which there was but little done, that season. Mr. Wood,[3] with a prospecting party discovered, at the same time, Wood's Creek on the Stanislaus, out of which the few who were there then were realising between two and three hundred dollars per day, with a pick and knife alone.

Carson,[4] who had been directed by an Indian, discovered what has since been known as Carson's Creek, in which himself and a small party took out, in ten days, an average of 180 ounces each. Angel[5] also discovered Angel's Creek, at which he wintered in 1848. Ever first with the discoveries were Capt. Weber's trading stores—John and Daniel Murphy, and Dr. Isabell being with them. With many traders, in those days, weighing gold for Indians and white people was a different matter: honesty, generosity, and justice marked their

1. Sutter hired Indians to work these diggings in 1848—now the town of Sutter Creek.
2. Apparently this is Dry Creek, at or near present-day Drytown, on highway 49.
3. A common name. This particular Wood probably was a prospector who came from Oregon, found gold and left his name on this creek, and was flayed alive by Indians in January 1851.
4. James H. Carson, the author, is referring to himself.
5. Henry Angel, a prospector for Weber, left his name upon the creek and on the town of Angels Camp.

James Marshall, the discoverer of gold at Sutter's mill.

every transaction with the christian—but they had weights and prices for the Indians. And if this should meet the eyes of any of them, they will please receive the thanks of the writer for teaching him the art of *throwing the lead,* for the benefit of the Digger Indians.

The gold discoveries reached no farther south during 1848 —with the exception of the Tualumne, on which gold was known to exist, only. The rains commenced the last of October, which drove full two thirds of the diggers out to the towns on the coast, where we will follow them directly. Those who remained in the mines, during the winter of '48, made but little at mining, as the supplies for their subsistence were so high as to absorb all they made—but the traders amassed fortunes.

In 1846 and '47, the price of the finest horses was $20; fat bullock, $6; wild mares, 75 cents each; flour and vegetables—"we hadn't had any." We lived on beef and beans—beef dried, fried, roasted, boiled and broiled morning, noon, and night—as much as every man wanted—without money or price; with a change, at times, of elk, venison, and bear steak. The emigration of 1846 did not expect to find any luxuries in California—with the exception of a balmy atmosphere and a rich soil—and they well knew that industry would soon supply the rest. The discovery of gold raised the price of gold in proportion with everything else. Horses and mules in the mines were worth from two to four hundred dollars; cattle from one to two hundred dollars per head. I have seen men give two and three hundred dollars for mules and horses—ride them from one diggings to another—take their saddles off and set the animals loose, never looking for them again—remarking, "that it was easier to dig out the price of another, than to hunt up the one astray."

The morals of the miners of '48 should here be noticed. No man worked on Sunday *at digging* for gold; but that day was spent in

prospecting in the neighborhood by the
more sedate portion of the miners; while
others spent it in playing at poker, with
lumps of gold for checks; others collected
in groups, might be seen under the shade
of neighboring trees, singing songs, playing at old sledge[6] and drinking whisky; in
all of which proceedings harmony, fun and
good will to each other was the prominent
feature. We had ministers of the gospel
amongst us, but they never preached.

Sutter's mill.

Religion had been forgotten, even by its ministers, and instead of
their pointing out the narrow paths that led to eternal happiness to
the diggers, "on each returning Sabbath morn," there they might be
seen with pick-axe and pan travelling untrodden ways in search of
"filthy lucre" and treasure that "fadeth away," or drinking good
health and prosperity with friends.

---

6. A card game for two or three players, also called *all fours, high-low-jack, pitch,*
    and *seven-up.*

A Miner's Burial

The only religious service I ever saw undertaken in the mines in '48 was at a miner's funeral on the South Fork. Amongst the miners was one who was known as "the Parson." Those who were acquainted with him asserted that the Parson had "onst" been a "powerful preacher" in the Eastern States; but digging for gold had greatly tarnished his Gospel habiliments; in short, he had become *carnal*, and would take a big drink with any of his friends he met. A miner had died who was much liked, and we determined to give him as respectable a funeral as circumstances would permit. The parson was requested to officiate as minister on the occasion, which he readily assented to, and soon made his appearance at the camp of the deceased—where a goodly number were collected, amongst whom tin cups passed swiftly around, and many a drink went down to the repose of the soul departed.

The Parson never missed a "round," and by the time we got the corpse to the grave, he had become somewhat "muddled." The grave had been dug in a flat some hundreds of yards from the camps. After the body had been placed in the grave, the miners gathered around it, and the Parson read a long chapter from the Bible, after which he said it was necessary to sing a Psalm. No hymn book could be procured—and no one had ever committed a hymn to memory, with the exception of the Parson, who soon started one, to the tune of "Old Hundred." He got through the first verse, and the first line of the second, and there *stuck*. After several ineffectual and comical attempts to "start her" again, he coolly informed us that the Lord had obliterated from his memory the balance of that solemn psalm, but we would go to prayer. At the order for prayer, some remained standing—numbers knelt around the grave—and one *old case* sat down, remarking, at the time, that he "knew when the Old Parson had his steam a little up, he was h—l on a prayer; and he was going to take it easy." The Parson had been praying some ten minutes, when some of those kneeling around the grave commenced examining the dirt that had been thrown up, and found it to be (as they expressed it) "Lousy with gold." This discovery necessarily created an excitement in the assembly. The Parson had become "warmed up"— and his supplications for the soul of the departed could be heard

"Echoing through mountain, hill, and dell,"

when he suddenly stopped—opened one eye—and looked down to see
what was disturbing his hearers, and very coolly enquired, "Boys
what's that?" "Gold! by G–d!—and the richest kind o' diggin's!—the
very dirt we have been lookin' for!" The truth flashed across his
mind—then he raised his hands, and with a comic expression of countenance, informed us that the 'congregation are dismissed,' as it was
highly necessary that *that* dirt should be well tried before we proceeded any farther, and away he "scud" for his pan.

Suffice it to say that poor George B—— was not buried there, but
was taken from his *rich hole*, and a grave made for him "high up the
mountain's side."

Now let us look at the coast cities, and the settlements during '47
and '48. The first emigration to California from the U.S. took place in
1846. Many persons perished in the mountains, or were compelled to
subsist on the flesh of their dead companions. These men—enured to
toil—knowing no fear—with hearts that had grown big with the love
of freedom, soon hoisted a Flag of Independence, determined to build
up a Republic on the Pacific. The war with Mexico brought to our
shores the broad stripes and bright stars of America. The *Bear Flag*
was hoisted, and beneath it, under Col. Fremont and other brave
officers, were soon enrolled those sons of the forest who followed
their leaders against the enemy through the hard winter of '46.
Their hardships and sufferings through that campaign were un-
equaled by any during the war with Mexico. At Los Angeles, in
the spring of '47, they were disbanded, without pay for services or
remuneration for supplies furnished by them—and, like our fathers
of the revolution, they returned to their homes, naked and destitute.

Exploring for Gold

BUT LITTLE PROGRESS WAS MADE in agricultural pursuits during '47. In the spring of 1848, considerable crops were sown, of wheat in particular. San Francisco, Monterey and San Jose were fast improving under the head of industry, and many comfortable buildings were erected. Sonoma and Santa Cruz were also becoming settled. The discovery of the gold mines put an entire stop to these improvements. The towns were deserted, ranches with their crops ungathered were left to the mercy of thousands of cattle and horses, with which the valleys and hills were then covered. The ravens croaked from the house-tops, and grass grew around the doors of the rancherias.

The gold discoveries were made known to the departments at Washington by Col. Mason—his reports to the departments were taken up by that lever of all greatness, the press. Its thousand tongues proclaimed it to the world, and a mania seized the civilized of every land. A revolution of affairs took place that naught but gold could effect; and every man set face towards the land of Ophir. Oregon furnished the first emigrants, Chili and Sonora next—and the balance of creation soon followed. At the close of 1848 our population consisted of about ten thousand. We promised to follow the miners to the towns on the coast, where about two-thirds had gone to winter. San Francisco, Monterey and Los Angeles had received the greater portion of this heterogeneous mass, men ragged and filthy in the extreme, with thousands of dollars in their pockets, filled the houses and streets, drinking and gambling away their piles. No supplies or accommodations could be obtained. In San Francisco in particular, every house and tent was nightly crowded with these beings, who were in many cases packed away in rooms like shad. I applied at a public house in San Francisco in October for food and lodgings—I got beef broiled, hard bread, and a cup of awful coffee, for which I paid the moderate sum of five dollars. By furnishing my own blankets and paying a dollar, I got permission to sleep on a bowling alley, after the rolling had ceased, which was near two o'clock in the morning. Gambling seemed to be the ruling passion—there was no value set on money, as it would not procure the comforts of life, or amusement or pleasure to the holders; millions of dollars were recklessly squandered at the gaming tables and drinking shops. As soon as a miner became *flat broke*, he wended his way to the mines again, to replenish his pile, and have another *bust*. Some few, as soon as they procured eight or ten thousand dollars, availed themselves of the first opportunity, and left for more quiet lands. I have seen men with from thirty to fifty thousand dollars worth of dust, shipping as sailors before the mast, for ports in the Pacific, from which they could reach the U.S.

Winter in San Francisco. (Marryat, *Mountains and Molehills*.)

The price of labor had risen with everything else, and wages ranged from sixteen to forty dollars per day, according to the nature of the employment, and men could not be had, in most cases, at those rates. I remember seeing the captain of a brig on the beach at San Francisco, who had a crew with the exception of a cook; he met a negro and asked him if he wished to go as cook for him on his brig;— the negro, after cocking his hat on the side of his head, and bringing his arms akimbo, coolly inquired the wages offered. The captain informed him that ten dollars per day was as much as he could afford. The negro, at this offer, burst into a loud laugh, and informed the captain, "Dat if de *capten* wished to hire he seff out for twenty dollars a day to fil dat occupation, jus walk up to de restaurant, and he would set him to wock immediately." The negro had to leave—and California, its people, and the negroes in particular, received a cursing, such as sailors only know how to give.

Col. Mason, the military Governor, was left without servants or cooks, and I have known him to be discussing State affairs, and at the same time agreeably employed cooking *flap jacks*, of which not the slightest notice was taken; as everybody knew that such things in those days had to be.

Laws to govern us, we had none, with the exception of the laws of usage, called by those who do not know its purifying influence in a new population, Lynch Law. The laws of Mexico were *presumed* to exist, but were not enforced but by the consent of all parties concerned, in civil cases. We had Alcaldes who we elected, or they occupied their offices by appointment from the Governor. To the decision of these, trifling disputes were given as final. But if theft, robbery or murder were committed, we threw down our mining tools, shouldered our rifles, and the offending parties were soon on trial before a jury; if he was found guilty, he then and there paid the penalty; if innocent, he was dismissed with an admonition. I believe there was but one case of these high misdemeanors tried in 1848—a Frenchman had become notorious for horse stealing in the neighborhood of the dry diggings—his propensity for horse and mule flesh became so great, that it attracted the attention of the miners, and we determined to put a stop to it. He was soon caught in the very act of horse stealing, brought in and tried, and in two hours after he was taken, he was dangling between heaven and earth, at the end of a rope. This severe but just punishment put a stop to thieving exploits, until '49, where we will mention it again.

The first exploring parties for the discovery of gold to the south of where the discovery of '48 rested, was in the month of March, 1849. The Mission Indians of San Miguel had brought into Monterey large specimens of gold, and reported it to have come from King's River and its vicinity.[1] Mr. William R. Gardner, who had been in California for some fifteen years, and was acquainted with some of these Indians, determined to fit out a trading expedition for that region; the writer of this was importuned to accompany him, but owing to the indefensive manner in which he persisted in going, the offers were declined. Gardner left Monterey the 1st of March, with five or six ox wagons, with Indian drivers and four Spaniards as companions; he passed through the coast range at the pass of San Miguel, crossed the lake slough near the Tulare Lake, and then passed up the north side of King's river to the foot of the Sierra Nevada; here he was met by Indians in large numbers from the mountains, who displayed large quantities of gold; they refused to trade with him unless he came to their settlements; they having every mark, apparently, of friendship for him, he travelled two days into the mountains, where the Indians attacked him, killing himself and all his party, with the exception of a Sonoranean who was accompanying them. This man brought back nothing of Mr. Gardner's property, with the exception of his papers, amongst which was his journal of the expedition. In his last entrys, he says: "We have travelled about twenty miles to day, the number of Indians around us have increased every hour for the last three days, and now number over a thousand—most of them have gold, which is generally coarse, and to my enquiries of them where they obtained it, they point to the eastward. There is a great stir amongst the Indians, and their squaws and children have left. I have now the greatest fears for my safety." Here the journal ended, leaving doubts on the mind of the actual existence of gold in the region he had visited. The Indians who murdered Gardner and party,

---

1. In 1805 a Spanish exploring expedition named this river *Rio de los Santos Reyes*, the River of the Holy Kings. This was later anglicized into Kings River, but for a time it was called King's River, as though named for a man named King.

were the Chochillas, Chowochimincs and Cowies[2]—the most thieving, treacherous and blood-thirsty tribes of the Tulares.

The next exploring party consisted of Messrs. Loveland, Curtis,
Harris, Swain and some four others. This party reached the mountains on the 20th of March, some fifteen miles above the Merced
river, and made the first discovery of gold in the neighborhood of
what is now known as Burn's diggings; but before they had made
any progress, the Indians attacked them in large numbers, drove
them out, and dangerously wounded two of their party.

The next party of exploration were more formidable than the two
first mentioned. This party consisted of ninety-two men, under the
guidance of Carson & Robinson,[3] of Monterey; they were composed
of dragoons and discharged teamsters from the command of Major
Graham, which had arrived from Mexico, and a number of disbanded
volunteers of Col. Stephenson's[4] regiment, well armed and equipped.
The party struck into the Sierra Nevada where the Mariposa enters
the plains, and explored the adjacent country, finding gold in many
places; they thence proceeded to the Merced and Tuolumne and found
gold on these streams and tributaries as far as they went. The reports of these expeditions soon peopled these regions. Col. Fremont
and his party were about the first who dug for gold in the Mariposa
region on what is known as Fremont's creek.

---

2. Chowchillas (Chauchilas), Choinimni, and Kaweahs (Ga'wia), three of the Yokuts
   tribes that inhabited the San Joaquin (Tulares) Valley. The Choinimni lived on the
   Kings River, and thus probably were the ones who killed Gardner.
3. James H. Carson, the author, and probably George Robinson, a sergeant in
   Stevenson's First Regiment of New York Volunteers.
4. Jonathan D. Stevenson. In 1849 he bought the Rancho Los Medanos and laid out
   the site of a town, where Pittsburg now is, which he called the "City of New York
   of the Pacific," after his home city.

Jonathan D. Stevenson. (*The Annals of San Francisco.*)

The Mines in '49

Nот BEING PLEASED with the discoveries south, I started back
with a small party to the scenes of my former good fortunes; but
when I arrived, 1st May, 1849, a change had come over the scene
since I had left it; Stockton, that I had last seen graced only by Joe
Buzzel's log house with a tule roof, was now a vast linen city. The
spiral masts of barques, brigs, and schooners were seen high pointed
in the blue vault above—while the merry "ye ho" of the sailor could
be heard, as box, bale, and barrel were landed on the banks of the
slough. A rush and whirl of noisy human beings were continually
before the eye. The magic wand of gold had been shaken over a desolate place, and on it a vast city had arose at the bidding.

The winter of '48 and spring of '49 had brought to our shores an
addition of some fifty thousand to our population. Sacramento city,
like Stockton, had sprung up Minerva like, full grown; Sutter's Fort
was nearly deserted, or at least no trade was carried on within its
walls; Sacramento and Stockton had then become, and ever will
remain the great depots for the mining regions.

We continued on to the old diggings from Stockton. When we
reached the top of the mountains overlooking Carson's and Angel's
creeks, we had to stand and gaze in silence on the scene before us—
the hill-sides were dotted with tents, and the creeks filled with
human beings to such a degree that it seemed [as] if a day's work of
the mass would not leave a stone unturned in them. We did not stop,
but proceeded on to Wood's creek, in hopes to there find more room
to exercise our digging propensities. But here it was worse—on the
long flat we found a vast canvass city, under the name of Jamestown,[1] which, similar to a bed of mushrooms, had sprung up in a

---

1. Named for Colonel George F. James, who settled on Woods Creek in 1848.

night. A hundred flags were flying from restaurants, taverns, rummills, and gaming houses. The gambling tables had their crowds continually, and the whole presented a scene similar to that of San Francisco during the past winter. I have there seen Spaniards betting an aroba of gold at a time, and win or lose it as coolly as if it had been a bag of dirt. Gold dust had raised in value to what it was in '48—as high as ten dollars per oz. was given for it at the monte banks. Wood's creek was filled up with miners, and I here for the first time after the discovery of gold, learned what a *miner's claim* was. In '48 the miners had had no division of the ground into claims— they dug where it was richest, and many times four or five could be seen at work in a circle of six feet in diameter; but here they were now measuring the ground off with tape measures, under the direction of the Alcaldes, so as to prevent disputes arising from the division.

In the great emigration that had taken place, the city and state of New York had the majority against the balance of the states; and although the greater part of them were gentlemen and good hearted fellows, yet there were some of the smallest specimens of the human family amongst them that I ever saw in California. I have seen some of these arrive in the diggings, and in their settlements quarrel about four cents difference. A man who would quarrel in the gold mines of California in 1849, about such an amount, certainly must have had a soul so small that ten thousand of them would not make a shadow.

Mormon Gulch,[2] Soldiers' Gulch,[3] Sullivan's Diggings,[4] and the Rich Gulch[5] of the Moquelumne, had been rich discoveries, made during the fall and winter, and were now centres of attraction. Curtis's creek[6] and the rich diggings of the flats around Jamestown soon followed. In October, '48, a small party of us were encamped on

---

2. The original name for Tuttletown.
3. A town that has disappeared. It was about a mile west of Jackass Hill; the gulch runs into the Stanislaus River just south of highway 49.
4. Also now gone. John Sullivan was a native of Ireland who came to California in 1844 with the Stevens party. Highway 108 crosses Sullivan Creek a mile east of Sonora.
5. There were two camps named "Rich Gulch" in Calaveras County. This is probably the one five miles northeast of Mokelumne Hill.
6. This vanished camp was about three miles south of Sonora.

the flat where Sonora now stands. Nightly a California lion greeted us with his long howl, on the hill now occupied by the town; he seemed to be conscious that the white man was approaching, and that his old play-grounds were soon to be occupied by a tented city.

The northern mines had also received a heterogeneous mass to their population, and towns were springing up through the mineral districts. Coloma, like the rest, had grown up in a day, but more substantial than her sisters, being principally frame buildings. The timber for these buildings was sawed on the ground, being taken at the saw mill at five hundred dollars per thousand feet.

Each day now added thousands to our population; all of whom came intent on making fortunes in a few days and then leaving the country; many came on speculating expeditions; property of every description ran up to rates that set the world to wondering. In San Francisco in particular, lots and buildings changed hands at rates unknown before in the annals of trade.

I. Thou shalt have no other claim than one. (James M. Hutchings, *The Miners' Ten Commandments*.)

But to return to the diggings. This swarm of human beings laid cold the bright calculations of the old diggers of 1848. They had found gold at every step, and looked on the supply as inexhaustible—that for years to come few would be here, and that our rich harvest would continue as it then was. Men who would work could get from one to five hundred dollars per day, and in confidence of this good fortune continuing, these heavy earnings were foolishly spent in drinking and gambling, purchasing fine horses, and dressing in gaudy Indian style. Honesty was the ruling passion of '48. If an *hombre* got broke, he asked the first one he met to loan him such amounts as he wanted, until he could *dig her out*. The loans were always made, and always

II. Thou shalt not make unto thyself any false claim, nor any likeness to a mean man, by jumping one; whatever thou findest on the top above or on the rock beneath, or in a crevice underneath the rock;—or I will visit the miners around to invite them on my side; and when they decide against thee, thou shalt take thy pick and thy pan, thy shovel and thy blankets, with all that thou hast, and "go prospecting" to seek good diggings; but thou shalt find none. Then, when thou hast returned, in sorrow shalt thou find that thine old claim is worked out, and yet no pile made thee to hide in the ground, or in an old boot beneath thy bunk, or in buckskin or bottle underneath thy cabin; but hast paid all that was in thy purse away, worn out thy boots and thy garments, so that there is nothing good about them but the pockets, and thy patience is likened unto thy garments; and at last thou shalt hire thy body out to make thy board and save thy bacon. (James M. Hutchings, *The Miners' Ten Commandments*.)

paid, according to promise. The writer, on one occasion, was accosted at the old dry diggings, by name, by a rough looking case, but with whom I had no acquaintance, for the loan of some dust until a specified time. His rough hands and muscular arms proclaimed him to be a working man, which was all the security required. Without asking his name, the amount (fifty ounces) was handed to him. On the day appointed, it was duly returned, with an additional *pound*, and a bottle of brandy for old acquaintance' sake, as he remarked, telling the lender at the same time that he considered him a d——d fine *feller*. It would not be very safe to let out dust under the same circumstances at the present date.

But this honesty, so universal in '48, was not to be found in the crowds that daily thickened around us in '49. Hordes of pick-pockets, robbers, thieves and swindlers were mixed with men who had come with honest intentions. These rascals had lived all their lives by the "sleight of hand," and it was evident that they had not come to California with gold rings on their white soft hands, for the purpose of wielding the pick and pan in obtaining their wishes. Murders, thefts and heavy robberies soon became the order of the day. A panic seized that portion of the diggers, who never before had been out of the sight of marm's *chimbly*, and who went cringing about in fear, although most of them presented the appearance of travelling armories; yet it was evident they wouldn't shoot. But men were to be found who had ridden the "Elephant" of this world all their lives, and knew well the course we had to pursue under the change of affairs. Soon whipping on the bare back, cutting off ears, and hanging, became matters of as frequent occurrence as that of robbery, theft and murder.

The civilized world may cry down the short but concise code of Judge Lynch, but I feel confident that every honest man in California has hailed it as a God blessed evil to them. If a depredation was committed, the long rifles of the honest boys were

III. Thou shalt not go prospecting before thy claim gives out. Neither shalt thou take thy money, nor thy gold dust, nor thy good name, to the gaming table in vain; for monte, twenty-one, roulette, faro, lansquenet and poker, will prove to thee that the more thou puttest down the less thou shalt take up; and when thou thinkest of thy wife and children, thou shalt not hold thyself guiltless—but insane. (James M. Hutchings, *The Miners' Ten Commandments.*)

slung across their shoulders, and the depredator was soon ferreted out and brought to trial before a jury, where every chance was allowed the accused to prove himself innocent—if he was found guilty, his punishment was awarded by the jury, and the sentences, whatever they were, immediately put in execution. Petty thefts and frauds were punished by inflicting on the culprit from 50 to 200 lashes with a raw-hide on his bare-back, laid on according to the directions in the *code*. If the offence was stealing horses, mules, oxen or large amounts of gold dust, death was always awarded; and hundreds of the bodies of these rascals who came to California to steal, because we had no law, now lay rotting in felons' graves.

IV. Thou shalt not remember what thy friends do at home on the Sabbath day, lest the rememberance may not compare favorably with what thou doest here. Six days thou mayest dig or pick all that thy body can stand under; but the other day is Sunday; yet thou washest all thy dirty shirts, darnest all thy stockings, tap thy boots, mend thy clothing, chop thy whole week's firewood, make up and bake thy bread, and boil thy pork and beans, that thou wait not when thou returnest from thy long-tom weary. For in six days' labor only thou canst not work enough to wear out thy body in two years; but if thou workest hard on Sunday also, thou canst do it in six months; and thou, and thy son, and thy daughter, thy male friend and thy female friend, thy morals and thy conscience, be none the better for it; but reproach thee, shouldst thou ever return with thy worn-out body to thy mother's fireside; and thou shalt not strive to justify thyself, because the trader and the blacksmith, the carpenter and the merchant, the tailors, Jews, and buccaneers, defy God and civilization, by keeping not the Sabbath day, nor wish for a day of rest, such as memory, youth and home, made hallowed. (James M. Hutchings, *The Miners' Ten Commandments.*)

We were not blessed at that day with statutes as unintelligible as a Chinese bible, or with hordes of lawyers, who, for a pittance, would screen, under the informalities of indictments or proceedings, villains from just punishment. There were no jails or prison ships; but if a culprit was taken, he never escaped—money or influence availed him nothing. If he attempted escape, the unerring rifle brought him to a sudden halt. I am not an advocate of unlawful trials by the people; but those who know the purifying influence of Judge Lynch in 1849, and of the vigilance committee in 1851, will join with me in saying that their institution and their firm devotion to the cause of right, alone saved California from becoming the theatre of strife and bloodshed unknown before in the history of the world.

The Law, Physic, the Press

OWING TO THE MASS OF BEINGS in the mines in '49, it became necessary for us to have alcaldes and sheriffs for the different mining districts, who were elected to office by a majority of the miners. They formed courts, before which culprits were brought; they also settled disputes arising out of disputed claims. They had no enacted laws to govern their actions, but what they thought was right was the law; but most cases of petty criminal offences and cases of disputes were left to a jury, who were summoned by the alcalde. The alcalde's fee, in all cases, was three ounces; sheriff's, two; and each juror one—with the addition of the price of all the whiskey used by the court, jury and witnesses during the trial; if it was a criminal offence the prisoner had to foot the bill, if he was worth it, if not, no pay was required; but in all other cases the parties had to *pungle down the dust* in advance, or they got no law. As an instance of settling small disputes at the alcalde's courts, I will mention one or two in which I was summoned as a juror. At the rich gulch, on the Moquelumne, in the spring of '49, two Spaniards who were known to have had great luck in digging *oro*, had a dispute about the ownership of an old mule, worth about $20, and applied to the alcalde to settle the matter between them; his honor informed them, that before he could extend the great arm of the law over them they would each have to *fork* over three ounces for the expenses, which was done without a murmur—each commenced his harangue as to the ownership—not one word of which was understood by the court. After matters had thus progressed for a short time, his honor informed them, in good English, that they had better leave it to the decision of a jury. This was interpreted to them, and they gladly availed themselves of the offer. Two ounces more was paid in advance to the sheriff, before he would summon a jury. A jury of twelve men were soon collected, and the case brought before them. Neither of the parties could produce

evidence that the mule had belonged to them; and the jury, after hear-
ing their statements, retired, and soon returned into court with their
verdict, which was that the plaintiff and defendant pay each an equal
share of the cost of court, and then *draw cuts* for the mule in dispute.
The alcalde's, sheriff's and juror's fees amounted to twenty ounces,
and the *liquor bill* to three ounces. This the Spaniards cheerfully
paid, drew *straws* for the mule, and went on their way rejoicing.

An Alcalde at the mines examining a lump of gold—catches the fever—drops his staff of
office, and tells his sheriff to go home and hang the prisoner whom he left at the bar, and
he will sentence him afterwards. (Colton, *Three Years in California.*)

Another instance, illustrative of the times, was a trial between
two Jews, at Carson's Creek. These two sons of Israel had carried on
a shop in partnership, and had realized a fortune, but in their settlement there was twenty-two hundred dollars in dispute between
them, and it was given to the alcalde for settlement, and he referred
it to the decision of a jury. The miners knew that the *gents* had real-

ized their *pile* off the labor of others, and were determined that the
litigants should at least *pay* for all the *law* they received. The first
jury disagreed—another was called—that also could not decide;
a third was made up, who came to an agreement, which was—that
the expenses of the whole trial should first be paid, and then the
remainder equally divided between the two Jews. The *bar*—not of
the court, but of the rum-mill attached—had been thronged during
the day, which bill, of course, was to be paid by the disputants. The
bill of cost was soon made up, and amounted to *eighteen hundred
dollars.* This the Jews refused to pay; but the verdict of the jury and
the money were both in the hands of the alcalde, and he informed
them that his *oath of office* compelled him to execute the jury's decision; he therefore paid from their bag the cost, and equally divided
between them the remainder. They did *not* "go their way rejoicing,"
but went off swearing a string of Hebrew curses, which portended
no good to the law-givers.

We have noticed cases of *Law* and *Gospel* in the early scenes of
the golden days, and it would be slighting Æsculapius if we were to
pass *Physic* by unnoticed. Of skillful physicians, we had none in the
mines. It is true there were some who had been hospital stewards
of the army and navy, and others who had been druggists in other
lands; but none who could be pronounced *scientific.* In the fall of '48,
portions of the northern mines were unusually sickly, and those who
remained on the rivers during August and September of that year
(if they were not too lazy to shake,) had the fever and ague. A man
who got sick suffered; there was no shelter for him; no attention paid
his wants; nor could medical aid, in many instances, be procured.
Thus situated—suffering from disease and neglect—exposed to the
hot sun during the day, and cold nights—many died. I met a poor
fellow from Feather river, who was trying to reach Sutter's Fort;
his teeth were chattering together, and his whole frame was in a
pleasing shake. On enquiry, he informed me that every body on the
river was as bad as he was, and he only left because "the *pine bushes*
had taken the *ager,* and were dying so fast that he thought he had
best make his escape."

If such a thing as a doctor could be procured, his charges for the
medicine and advice were in unison with everything else of the
times—an ounce of dust was to be paid for each thing he done. If he

came to see a patient, felt his pulse, looked at his tongue, and asked the *state of his bowels*, the charge was four ounces, and an ounce per dose for any medicine he administered—if nothing more than a dose of salts. Medicines were scarce—quinine in particular—for which I have frequently seen ten dollars per grain given.

In these *Early Recollections* the press has been neglected, or rather unnoticed. In 1846 the first newspaper ever printed in California, in the English language, was issued at Monterey—printed on paper used by the Spaniards in the manufacture of their cigaritos. It was edited by R. Semple and Walter Colton, and called "The Californian." It was removed to San Francisco in the spring of '47 where it took the name of "The Alta California," which it has ever since retained, and is now one of the largest and most widely circulated daily papers in the State. At the time of the discovery of the gold mines its editions were laboring along, honestly making all they could with their *little sheet*, but the fell destroyers, the *gold fever*, could not even spare to the people their only source of information, the little *Alta*. Its editors and proprietors struggled hard to keep it up; but at length its columns informed its patrons, that that would be its last appearance for some time, as its compositors, pressman, *devil* and all, had left for the mines, and its editors could stand it no longer. Soon after an observer might have seen the last representative of the Alta snugly stored on board a launch, wending his way up the Sacramento. The little paper did not die, but "slept;" and no great time elapsed before its *bechalked shingle* was again swinging in the gentle zephyrs which played at times around the hills of *Yerba Buena*. Its proprietors found that it was full as easy to set type as to rock the cradle, *Lucy*, on the waters of the American, and the Alta was soon amongst us again. It grew with California's greatness. At each prostration of San Francisco before the scathing hand of fire it could be seen rising from its ashes.

True Love, Sailors, and the Dandy

A FEW SKETCHES FROM LIFE IN THE DIGGINGS in '48 and '49, may here prove interesting. The fortunes being daily made by labor in the mines induced men of every profession and calling to take the pick-axe and pan; mingled together in the search for gold was to be seen Ex-Governors, members of Congress, lawyers, doctors, mechanics of every grade, merchants, men delicate, and men inured to trial, and representatives of every people on earth. Amongst such a community, the observer of human nature had a wide field for study. The lust for, and the struggles to obtain the wealth of this world, often shows up human nature in all its deformities. In some its acquirement brings out the good part of our nature, and men who were looked upon while poor, as savages towards their fellow-men, prove under the influence of wealth, pure philanthropists and brothers to the human family; but such cases are of rare occurrence. The effect of sudden wealth on mankind, has, perhaps, never been so deeply marked as in California. I have here seen men leaving the settlements in '48 poor and nearly naked for the mines; these men were then the comrades of poor, but honest men, who, like themselves, had labored long in the eastern States without gaining a competence; after reaching the mines fortune followed them, one success after another had placed them, in the course of a few months, in possession of hundreds of thousands of dollars. This wealth, suddenly acquired, made them what the world are pleased to call *gentlemen,* in which situation, they looked on old companions in disdain, because they were poor, and often passed them with a cool nod of recognition. This was noticed in but very few cases amongst the old settlers, on whom the effect of wealth had not the power to change their natures.

I worked in Carson's creek near a party of men from Oregon. Some were men of family—others had left sweethearts behind; and one of them, a young man, appeared to have no other design than to

make happy his aged parents. I learned that his parents were aged,
helpless, and depended entirely on the exertions of their son for
subsistence. He had struggled hard to make them comfortable; but
low wages, and high prices for all he purchased, had kept him from
making much progress, and he had now managed to reach California
over the mountains, with bright hope to illumine his path. When he
reached the diggings, *hope* and *doubt* could be seen struggling within
his soul. But a short time elapsed before his muscular arms were
swinging the pick; success must attend a cause like his; and soon his
heart was made glad by finding several large pieces; his countenance
beamed with delight; he had struck what miners term a rich pocket,
and as one chunk after another rolled out, his feelings would give
way in half maniac expressions; such as that's mam's, that's dad's,
that's for dad's winter coat, &c., as he worked without cessation.
Those who knew him said that he had made no other calculation than
for the comfort of his aged parents, if success attended his exertions.
In two days he had taken out nearly five thousand dollars, and then
bid us farewell for awhile; in his adieu to his companions, a tear could
be seen starting in his eyes, while his soul seemed to burst out in one
loud laugh, when he told them that he would go back and make his
parents rich and happy and then return again and work for himself;
and with him went the blessings of all around. Few men with a heart
like his had ever come to California without finding a rich pocket.

Amongst the same party was a love sick swain, whose marriage
had been prevented because he could not raise one hundred dollars
in money—a sum that his desired father-in-law required him to have
before he could get *his gal!* Most of the party knew these stipulations, and the frequent enquiry of Jake—"Have you raised the
hundred yet?" could be heard from some of the party every few
moments. Two or three days passed without Jake making any satisfactory answer, when one evening he took the proceeds of his labor
to a store and had it weighed, and found that he was the possessor
of nearly five hundred dollars. This was four times as much as he
thought he had, and it pleased him to such a degree that he came
pitching into camp like a young buffalo, and slapping his thighs with
his hands, and imitating the crowing of a cock, he exclaimed—"Wal,
boys, Jake's a married man now, by gosh." This raised a roar of
laughter throughout the camp. As soon as quiet was restored Jake

informed us "That he had 'bout five times as much as the old man *ever ax'd for the gal,* and he thought he would start back for Oregon to-morrow." This he was persuaded from doing before he had got enough to start house-keeping with. Three weeks after, Jake's "pile" had risen to over six thousand dollars, and great ideas of vast speculations filled his mind;—he had purchased some fine horses; threw away his buckskin suit, and was dressed in what he termed "fine store truck." One evening while we were around the camp fire, cooking slapjacks, frying pork, and preparing, in different ways, a *miner's supper,* Jake made his appearance amongst us. He appeared quite sedate, apparently in deep thought; but he was soon aroused by the enquiry of—"Jake, when are you going back to Oregon to marry your gal?" "Wal," said he, "I don't know as I'll go back to Oregon; and as to the gal, she's good enough, but you all know her old dad is purty darn'd poor, and I think I can do better some whar else;"—and I don't think Jake ever went back to claim his bride.

Men who left their families in Oregon to come to California for the purpose of improving their condition, generally set out for their homes with smiling faces, and manners and dispositions unchanged.

We had many sailor *diggers* amongst us, who had left their ships in distress in the bay of San Francisco. Jack is generally happy and jovial anywhere, but in the gold mines he was particularly so. One or two days work in the mines would give him the means of a good spree; and if they had clothes to wear, all they cared for was their *grub* and *rum,* which they freely indulged in, and all their earnings generally went to the shops; yet their jollity and proverbial good-heartedness never deserted them. If a man was unfortunate enough to be taken sick in the mines, he received but little attention; but with the sailors it was different. If one of them was taken sick his comrades paid him every attention until he recovered or died.

In the tide of emigration which set into the mines in the latter part of '48 and during '49, were to be found every species of the human family; and amongst the other animals, a full sized live *dandy* could be seen once in a while, with a very delicate pick, a wash pan made to order in the States, and a fine Bowie knife, perambulating through the diggings in search of "ah very rich hole, whah a gentleman could procure an agreeable shade to work under." Such cases as these, the old diggers generally made play-actors of, and gave them

the whole diggings for a stage on which to perform. The dandy has always been known to go dressed in the finest and most fashionable ap-
parel, kid gloves that covered lilly white hands, small walking stick,
hair usually long, and soaped down until his head shines like a junk
bottle, feet cased in patent leather boots, speaking a sweet little language of his own, which is faintly tinged in places with the English
tongue, was never known to have done an hour's work in his life, and
the oldest inhabitants never knew one of them to have a "dem cent."
Such a thing as that, of course, was never made for a *digger* in the
gold mines, although the old 'uns used to make them try it hard. One
of this species came into a ravine on the Stanislaus in which some
thirty men were at work; it was the month of June, '49, and the heat
of the sun was quite oppressive in the mountains, and most of us
were lying in our camps, but were aroused by the arrival of five
finely dressed strangers; four of them were professional men, who,
after having struggled hard for years in the Eastern States for a fortune without success, had come to California with the intention of
laboring in the mines; they were good-hearted fellows and gentlemen
in the true sense of the word; such as these, the old miners always
instructed, aided, and encouraged by every means, in their worthy
undertakings. The fifth one was a dandy, who, with his soft talk and
foolish questions, soon attracted the miners' attention, and his former companions (the four first mentioned) seemed to wish to get rid of
him. For the love of fun, we agreed to take him off their hands and in-
struct him in the fine art of handling the pick and spade. He was first
informed that he must get an axe, cut brush and build him a camp,
then to take off his fine shirt and a beautiful hat which was of that
pattern known as a *plug;* and a flannel shirt and straw hat offered
him in exchange. To this arrangement he could not submit, but informed us that he would not undergo such "ah dem transmogrifica-
tion—that he was ah gentleman—had been raised as such, and he
hoped we had common understanding sufficient to appreciate his feelings; that he had stopped amongst us because he knew we were 'dem
foin fellows,' and all he desired at present was to be given a rich hole,
very easy to dig." Such a place was shown him as was known to con-
sist of the hardest earth in the gulch, and where no gold had ever
been found. He set to work with his little pick, which he used about
as handy as a ring-tail monkey would. After working by spells for

A Dandy at the mines. (*Hutchings'*
California Magazine, July 1857.)

some two hours, he had thrown out about a bushel of dirt without seeing any gold. Disheartened, he threw down his tools, and came up to where some dozen of us were enjoying the rich sight of a "dandy's" first attempt at gold digging. He was in a perfect rage—swore that the gold mines were a "demed humbug—that Governor Mason had written positive falsehoods, for the purpose of enticing young men from their elegant homes to people this desolate region, and he deserved to be rode on a rail for his treachery." After he had blown off a long stream of fancy indignation gas, we advised him to cool down and go to work again, and he would have better success; to this he entered a *demurrer*, stating that he was a gentleman unused to such slavery; that it was impossible for him to subsist on such unpalatable food as we furnished him with; and being somewhat short of funds, he requested us to furnish him with dust sufficient to take him back to San Francisco, where he could get into business immediately. To this request, soft and gentle as it was, we told him that it was rather inconvenient for us to comply; but advised him to *hire* some men to work for him; that he could get good hands for $20 per day, who, he might rest assured, would get out each three ounces, thus giving him a fine profit. This seemed to please him well, and he set the next day as that on which his future fortunes were to commence. Early next morning he was to be seen making exertions to hire men to work for him, but without any apparent success, as he

soon came back and informed us that the "demed scoundrels had had
the impertinence to grossly insult him when he asked them to hiaw
out." At the bottom of the gulch, off from the rest, an old mountaineer had erected his brush house; and old trappers generally have
about the same regard for a dandy that he has for a skunk; and old
M—— was one of the oldest stamp, and was about as pleasant a
companion to mankind as a grizzly bear would prove to be. To M's
camp our dandy friend was directed, as being a place where he would
be sure to get one good man at least. After viewing his toilet for a
moment, off he started; the whole population of the hollow was on
tiptoe to know the result of his expedition. Some felt confident that
old M. would make him smell the muzzle of his rifle—others that he
would work for the dandy in a way that would be quite satisfactory
to a man of *feeling*. But a short time elapsed before a loud yell from
the vicinity of old M's camp, informed us that the beauty "vat wanted
to hire gold diggers" was in a tight place. What passed at M's camp
between the two, we never learned; but the yells drew nearer, until
at length the dandy and old M. were seen coming at rail-road speed;
M. had a brush from the side of his shanty, with which he gave the
dandy a loving rap at every jump; and as far as we could see them
over the hills, the same persuasive power of locomotion was being
applied. Old M. returned in a short time, swearing that "that ar
'tarnal varmint never come to his lodge without being sent thar,
and if he knew the man, he would have a lock of his 'har' to remember him by." We never saw our dandy digger again, and no doubt he
never stopped before San Francisco brought him up.

"Poor Quality"
and the "Prospector"

THE NEXT USELESS CLASS in the diggings, after the dandy, was what is known in the middle and southern states, as "Poor Quality." These were generally pitied, not despised. They were young men, sons of planters, who had once been wealthy, and had raised their sons up in idleness—taught them, in short, that it was low and despicable to labor—that labor was to be performed by slaves only, and was a dishonorable undertaking for a gentleman. But reverses of fortune often overtake us, and those possessing immense wealth, have seen it dwindling away without their possessing the power to prevent it. Slave after slave have been sold till all were gone, the old homestead divided among creditors, and the once wealthy planter sees around him a large family of sons and daughters who are dependent on relatives or friends for a continuation of their gentility. The sons of such as these I have here designated as "Poor Quality." Such young men as these, I have seen come into the mines where gold lay before them, and where they seemed to be determined to retrieve their fortunes by their own exertions. Unused to labor, or to endure any of the hardships of life, their tender constitutions were but illy calculated to stand the hardships attendant on the life of a miner in the Sierra Nevada. They generally possessed those high, noble principles so proverbial in the middle and southern states— brave, generous and good-hearted to a fault—they soon gained the good will of the old miners, who aided them in every way they could; but in their endeavors to dig for gold, their weak frames in a short time would sink beneath the toil; a few hours per day would be as much as they could work; and in many cases sickness would soon prostrate them. I have seen them laboring for a few moments, and then sit panting for breath for a long time before they could resume their work. If those who are now bringing their sons up in idleness and teaching them to despise labor, could but have seen these sights, and have heard the pitiful expressions of regret that often escaped from those noble youths, on their ignorance of labor and bodily weakness, to gain their desires, would change their policy without a further lecture on the subject. If these lines are ever read by men who are bringing up their sons in idleness, because the wealth of this world is at present heaped around them, I would pray of them to cease so despicable and destructive a policy towards their children. Teach them to work; raise them up to honest labor; for you cannot foresee the hour that *want* may make your sons curse you for your neglect.

But to return to the scenes in the mines. We will next notice one of the greatest curiosities of the diggings—a genius who always pleases himself, and amuses every body else; watch his manners— he is known as the "Prospector."

Prospecting (seeking new diggings) has been practiced more or less by every man that ever worked in the mines; some with great success, while others who have prospected ever since they reached the mines, have failed to make a single discovery. It would be for me to deny a well-known fact (though not a public one,) to say that the old miners did not all slightly believe in witchcraft;—luck, dreams, or in other words, a kind of *root chewing system*, for the discovery of rich placers, where piles were to be made in a short time. Prospecting parties have been the means of opening up to the world the riches of California.

In the early times of gold digging it was not so pleasant and easy to go on a prospecting expedition as it is at the present day. The regions of the Sierra Nevada, now peopled by thousands, and studded with large and thriving towns, was little over three years ago a howling wilderness, and untrodden by the foot of civilized man. It lay with its riches untouched and its value unknown, until the *prospectors* wended their way through these mountains, peopled by savages, made new discoveries, and proclaimed it to the world. Prospecting parties have been, and always will be, the means of developing the resources of the mineral lands of California, so far as placer diggings are concerned.

In describing the *prospector* here, I have reference only to such old *codgers* as have been *chewing roots*, and following different ideas as regards gold finding, ever since the first discovery was made, without any success. The first old genius of this kind I ever took particular notice of, was at the Old Dry Diggings. As I mentioned before, we all had ideas of our own in regard to finding rich places; but this old *hombre*, who had accidentally struck into a little ravine around which we were at work, and found it very rich, informed us that he possessed the power to find where all the richest places were; that he had found the present rich place by certain *divining* arts, of which he was master, and of course were to be known by him only. He worked but a short time before he informed us that much richer places were to be found. That night our old prospector was to be seen in his brush shanty, (at a comical light that he had made with the tallow of a bullock,) making suspicious looking circles, and odd looking marks on the ground. At times he consulted an old greasy pack of cards; at others, he would go out into the open air, and gaze long into the blue vault above, as if consulting some lucky planet for further information. At length, as if satisfied with his work, he rolled himself in his blankets and went to sleep. Not so with those who had been watching his manœuvres; they soon spread the sights they had seen (prodigiously lengthened,) throughout the neighborhood, and proved themselves more verdant than the old prospector, as they *sucked* the whole of his performance as a thing to be believed in. Many were the ideas formed in the minds of the diggers, and many expressions of disbelief, doubt and reliance were made, such as— "Ah, he's a d——d old fool—an old sucker, and no mistake. Who the d—l does he think believes in his witchcraft?" Others, bordering a little more on superstition, would say—"We don't know but the old fellow does possess such powers as he speaks of, for we read of such things as witches and wizards in the *Bible*. Yes, and I'll bet that that old fellow knows more than you think of;"—and many other such expressions were made. Next morning many eyes were slily watching his manœuvres. With his pick and knife, and head erect, the *prospector* started at an early hour for the adjacent hills. After first hunting apparently for some imaginary line on which he was to travel, and seeming to find it, he took a straight course; and to all enquiries made of him he maintained a dead silence. The only reply he would

make was by holding his finger up and gently shaking it, as if to en-
force silence, as he was *all right*. At night he returned, rather crest
fallen. The same party watched his motions that night again, which
consisted of the same performance as that of the past night.

A Prospector. (Marryat, *Mountains and Molehills*.)

Next morning he took a different direction, and was not gone over
an hour before he returned, packed his *kit* and left, loaded something
similar to a pack-mule. After him went a long line of diggers, believing that some rich discovery had been made. To all the enquiries
made of our old *gold finder*, he made no reply, only by suspicious
motions of his hands. After following him for about half a mile,
he came to a sudden halt, cast down his pack, took his pick and knife
up, looked at the sun, then took the bearings of the tops of some of
the neighboring pines, then with comic gestures and pantomimic
manners, gave his followers to understand that they were to remain
where they were for the present. He then started towards a ravine
near at hand. Stepping slow, soft, and as cautiously as if creeping

up on some wild game; at times he would stoop as if listening to sounds from the earth, then smilingly look back at the waiting crowd and place his finger on his mouth as if to enjoin silence, and then start again. During this part of the performance his followers were collected together in a group, with their countenances telling the workings of the inner man, some odd expressions at times escaping them, such as, "Wal, boys, that ar old cuss has something rich here;" an unbeliever doubted it; another would inform the crowd that those who placed no reliance in the thing, had better scud. The writer was there too, but I said nothing—didn't think much—but felt awfully streaked about that time. In short, a slight belief in necromancy was fast cooling off, and if there had been any way to have backed out, I should have taken it. Directly the old prospector reached the ravine; after picking out, carefully, a spot, his pick was raised, and descended into the hard earth. This was a signal for a general onset, and in a few moments over twenty picks were making the stones and iron earth fly in every direction, the closer to the wizzard the better. Not having any particular love for sinking holes through such earth as is to be found in some parts of the gold region, I concluded to let my pick rest until I could see some one get out a *chunk*. After waiting for some time, and no sign of gold yet appearing, my legs commenced certain quick movements towards the camp, in hopes that by an early arrival, no one would suppose that I had followed the wizzard.

The sun commenced sinking behind the western hills, and one after another of the believing diggers could be seen stealing their way back to camp, most of them by different ways from which they had left. All kept silent as regarded new discoveries, but a general understanding was made between the *sucked*, that they would not be alone. Gold bags were brought out, and every one put more or less in their pans, the amounts ranging from three oz. to three pounds, and dirt mixed with it as though it was the proceeds of their days' labor, and then taken in a stealthy manner to the water to be washed. Crowds of diggers gathered around, making all manner of inquiries about the new diggings, the direction they lay in, etc., to which questions, vague answers were given, but hints thrown out that something awful rich had been discovered by the old man of science. Sunrise next morning saw the woods alive with miners hunting for the new discovery; some failed to find our old prospector, and were out nearly all day; others soon found him, and soon returned to their work. To the enquiries of those that found his camp, and the numerous holes dug the day before, he informed them that he had missed the lead by a few feet, by some unaccountable miscalculation, but he would soon strike it. Curses deep and long were heaped on him and his science. A general good laugh all round, and the drinks at the old diggings, and the circumstance was soon forgotten.

At Woods' Creek, some two months after its discovery, where a great many of the miners from the old dry diggings were at work, we were astounded one day by the arrival of the old "Prospector," before mentioned. He had on his back his blankets, a change of clothing, pick-axe, shovel and pan—a frying-pan, coffee-pot and tin-cup, and about a week's provisions; he was welcomed by a *whoop* and a ha! ha! from all who knew him. After unpacking himself, he informed us that he had succeeded in following up the run of the rich gold-lead, all the way from the old diggings, but as it ran so deep he had not dug down to it but knew from the *blows* and other knowledge he was in possession of, that it must come to the surface of the earth at this place, and he had found it so. He was not alone, here, for there were several of the same stamp of *diviners* dodging about through the hills, whom the miners had ceased to follow.

General prospecting parties are too well known for a description of them to be interesting to the present community of California.

V. Thou shalt not think more of all thy gold, and how thou canst make it fastest, than how thou wilt enjoy it, after thou hast ridden rough-shod over thy good old parents' precepts and examples, that thou mayest have nothing to reproach and sting thee, when thou art left ALONE in the land where thy father's blessing and thy mother's love hath sent thee. (James M. Hutchings, *The Miners' Ten Commandments*.)

Digger Indians; the California cart

THE NEXT CLASS WE WILL NOTICE as being conspicuous in the early times of the mines, and who made vast fortunes for many, are the "Digger Indians."

The only thing that can be called *human* in the appearance of the digger Indians of the Sierra Nevada is their resemblance to the sons of Adam. I have made these class of beings a study and in them I find but few traits belonging to the human family.

In the early days of gold digging these Indians looked on in wonder at the exertions of the white men to procure from the rivers and gulches things not to be eaten, but they, following the examples of the whites, soon procured some for themselves and found that they could barter it for provisions and clothes. Indians were at work for miners and others, receiving in payment for a week's work an old shirt or handkerchief. The wild tribes were soon mingled amongst the whites in all the diggings. They came in from the *bug* and *acorn* hunting grounds, naked as nature had made them. Beef distributed amongst them had an attraction to bring them to the tents of the traders, whose slaves, in a manner, they became. All the gold they got was spent for such things as they took a fancy to. In their first trades, all they had in their possession was given, or offered, for any gewgaw that struck their fancy, as they had no idea of the value of gold. Thus it was that traders often received for a gaudy colored handkerchief, a fancy string of beads, or a red sash, from fifty to five hundred dollars. Whatever amount of gold was in possession of the Indian, he freely offered for such things as he pointed at. If it was accepted, he would snatch the article up, put down his gold, and go off jabbering like a monkey, at the idea of the manner in which he had *fooled* the white man. But this state of things did not continue long. Old Mission Indians informed them that the whites sold to each other by *ounces* and *pesos*, and that they could get more if they would have

their gold weighed. This opened the eyes of the traders, and some of
them procured scales and weights for the *accommodation* of the Indian while on his shopping expeditions. Whether the Indians gained
by the operation is rather doubtful. Indian prices of goods ranged
about as follows: cotton cloth or calico $20 per yard, plain white
blankets six ounces, serapes from twenty to thirty ounces each,
beads equal weight in gold, handkerchiefs and sashes two ounces
each, beef $5 per pound, and every thing else in like proportion. It
was not these prices only that they had to pay, as in settling, when
the scales and weights were brought out, to look at the slugs of lead
named pesos and ounces, and the arrangement of the scales, was
enough to make a white man blush; yet Mr. Indian regarded it as
perfectly fair, and would pile on gold until the scales would exactly
balance, using every precaution that he gave no more than the precise weight.

It was laughable to see the manner in which their fancy prompted
them to adorn themselves. Some taking a fancy to shirts, might be
seen parading around with a dozen on at a time; others decorated
themselves with red sashes and fancy handkerchiefs until they
resembled a decorated telegraph; while another portion thought a
Spanish hat sufficient to cover their entire nakedness—and in many
instances the wearer of the hat would have his naked heels adorned
with a huge pair of California spurs.

In July and August, '48, some of the settlers moved their families
into the mines, and the face of the American female was a new source
of wonder to the Indian race, and attracted them in large numbers.
Amongst the admirers of the white women, was one tall, fleshy,
well-formed Indian, who was as naked as he came into the world,
and he seemed to feel backward in going near them on this account,
but would stand behind a tree at some distance off, and peeping
from behind it, would admire them for hours at a time. At length he
seemed to have formed a resolution to dress himself, so that he could
approach nearer to them. For this purpose he went diligently to
work with a sharp stick, digging gold. He forsook his tribe, and was
ever to be found with white men. An everlasting smile was on his
face, and he appeared to be the soul of good nature. In a week he had
got a *pile* sufficient to dress himself up, and he wended his way to the
camp of a trader; here he purchased a uniform jacket, such as had

been worn by Col. Stevenson's regiment, a handkerchief, and a pair
of socks, and then commenced to dress up. The jacket was A No. 1,
and the man No. 4. When he buttoned it up the flesh stood out in a
roll around below it; the collar was so tight that it caused the veins
in his forehead to swell to the size of a man's finger; he then drew
on his socks, and made directly for the camps of the American ladies.
The jacket and socks were all that covered him, the rest of his person
being in a state of nature; but he felt sufficiently dressed for an inter-
view with the ladies, and he was soon amongst them, showing himself
off to the best advantage—but the pride of human nature is often
suddenly lowered—even that of digger Indians—for our beau was
unceremoniously kicked from the presence of the fair sex, by a very
rough looking *old dad.*

The reader is no doubt wearied by these descriptions of different
scenes in the mines. I will give a short description of the means of
transportation used in the early times of gold digging, and bring my
letters to a close.

At the time California was first occupied by the Americans, the
only means of transportation was in California carts and pack mules.
The California cart is a curiosity to the American when he first sees
it; it is like the California plough, an Egyptian invention, and may be
classed among the relics of antiquity. To those who have never seen
one, a short description may not be uninteresting. The wheels are
made by cutting blocks from the butts of the button-wood tree, are
about twenty inches in thickness, and from two to four feet in diameter; through this a hole for the axle is made, about six inches in
diameter; the axletree is made of a heavy oak timber; the tongue
or pole is usually about fifteen
feet in length, made of four by ten
scantling; to this is framed the
head of timbers of like size with
the pole; the body or box is made
of small poles, arranged round the
bed like a cage. In these unwieldy
things the rancheros transported
to the seacoast their hides and tallow, and lined with raw hides they
could transport barley or wheat;

A *carreta*, a California cart.

or by putting some beds in the bottom, and covering the top with a quilt or sheet, it was converted into a *pleasure* carriage, in which the Dons transported their lady friends to all places of amusement, or journeys of business. On these excursions the *carata* [*carreta*] was usually drawn by five or six yoke of oxen, driven by three or four Indians. The male portion of the family, mounted on fine horses, acted as escorts of honor, and the whole caravan was usually set off by some thirty to forty half starved dogs. With the exception of the few American wagons brought over by the Emigrants, these carts were the only locomotive power we had, and long trains of them could be continually seen on the roads leading from the southern country to the mines, from which they never returned, and in many cases never reached, as the numerous wrecks along the road testified. The speed of these machines was about twelve miles per day, provided they had not to stop to make new axletrees, which was usually to be done once per day at least. This means of transportation could not be depended upon for taking supplies into the mines; and those having American wagons would not commence making roads and hauling in supplies, while they could get from one to five hundred dollars per day by mining; and the only means for some time used was by pack mules. The price for transportation in launches on the rivers from San Francisco to Sutter's Embarcadero, was from 50 to 75 cents per lb., and from there to the mines was near the same price. Owing to the large supply usually taken in at first by the miners, there was not much transportation required until the winter of '48 and spring of '49, when the price of hauling from Stockton or Sacramento to the mines, ranged from $1 to $1.25 per pound. Provisions, in consequence, had to raise accordingly, and $200 for a bullock, $800 per bbl. of flour, and $400 per hundred lbs. for sugar, coffee and pork, were the prices we had to pay. These prices may sound as impossibilities to the miners of the present day—yet it is true. A great change has come over the scene—the times that were are now no more; gold is as plenty but not as easily got. In those times we picked it up from the top of the earth—now it is deep beneath the hills that hidden treasures are found.

Rich Resources,
and the Miners of '52

THE YEARS 1850 AND '51 HAVE PASSED. The world have stood amazed, and looked in wonder at the rapid strides to greatness that we have made. California has been admitted as a State—a civil government established. Cities and inland towns innumerable have sprung from chaos. The depths of the mountains have been made glad by the sound of busy life; the places desolate and lonely three years ago, are now graced by large and flourishing towns; a hundred steamers plough our waters, which had lain for ages unrippled by the hand of man; the plough-boy's merry whistle is heard as he turns up the rich soil, where, as if it were but yesterday, the elk and deer had their play-grounds. San Francisco, a city of four years growth, now spreads her bright wings o'er many hills, and laves her bosom far in the depths of the land-locked bay: several times in that short period have we seen her fair proportions laid in smoking ruins, and each time successively rebuilt, more bright, more great; and she now stands the proud emporium of the western seas. Vessels of every civilized nation of earth crowd her docks; and the bells of departing steamers scarcely cease to be heard. Yet, great as she is, her greatness is but just begun to what she is destined to become. Sacramento and Stockton, the great inland towns for trade and commerce, came into existence almost in a day. They, too, suffered from the scathing hand of flood and flame, but raised again e're the smoke of their destruction had died away.

The rich mineral and agricultural resources of our glorious young State is but just being developed; our rich soil, once pronounced barren and unfit for agricultural purposes is now yielding to the farmer its hundred fold, and our march is swift, onward and upward. Yet, amidst our present prosperity, there is a dark cloud that dampens the spirit of our enterprise—it is the indebtedness of our State, counties and city corporations.

Our civil government has been in existence but two years; our State is in debt *over two and a quarter millions of dollars;* our different counties, from ten to sixty thousand dollars; the corporations of the cities from five thousand to a million of dollars each. We have freely paid the enormous tax and licenses imposed upon us, and our indebtedness is daily increasing at a destructive rate. With the exception of San Francisco and Sacramento, we have not a jail or court house in the State; not one stone has been laid upon another by the State in the construction of a State House, State Prison, or any other building for the use of our government. Our laws are almost an enigma, and have failed to protect, as they should, the people.

The tax-payer very naturally inquires what has become of these vast sums? to what purpose have they been applied? whose pockets do they now fill? Our debts have been contracted by the representatives whom we have elected to office, and it makes no difference to what purposes the money has been applied, we stand pledged as an honorable people to pay it. *California will never repudiate.* Give us but five or six years to pay these debts, and it will be done without us feeling its burthen. Let our legislators lay aside all speculative schemes for one day, at least, and take the welfare of the people into consideration, and act in behalf of California's interests, so far as to *fund* the State debt, at an interest that *can* be paid; let them give the counties and corporations the same power, and the cloud that now sets upon our prospects will be cleared away.

Our only exports since the discovery of the gold mines of California has been *money.* Everything we consume, from the bread we eat to the handle of the miner's pick, has been imported at ruinous rates. Under these circumstances we cannot but be poor. The taxation for the support of our profligate government has been paid by the few; this has caused a dissatisfaction in one portion of the State, and a division of the *Western gem* is asked for.

Gentlemen, you have taken up your permanent residence in the land of gold, keep cool for a while, and you will have no cause for discontent. Let the land commissioners decide at the earliest day on the right to land claims which now have our agricultural energies bound down, and but a few months will intervene before the rich lands now lying idle will be in the hands of the agriculturist.

We have around us the sound of the mechanic's hammer and plane. Go to our valleys and at every step you will see the hand of the farmer scattering the bright seeds on our virgin soil, and the calm smile that plays across his honest, sun burnt face, assures you that his heart tells him of the return of an hundred fold. Two years more and California will cease to be a market for foreign products; we will have enough for our home consumption, and to spare. On the success or failure of our agricultural pursuits, depends the future wealth or poverty of California.

A word to the miners of the present day, and I am done. It is to you, *diggers*, I speak—you who are enduring the hardships and privations of the mountains, and working hard to honestly gain a fortune. Many of you, no doubt, are not making much more than what supports you comfortably, but a majority of you are getting more money per day for your labor than you could per week anywhere else in the civilized world; and you are happy, independent, and *your own masters*. A great many are yet realizing large fortunes in a short time. Don't any of you despair; there are yet just as rich diggings as ever have been discovered, and as large "chunks" beneath the earth yet as have ever been taken therefrom. It is true you have to work harder now to get it than formerly, yet it is to be had; thousands of square miles are yet lying untouched by the pick, beneath which millions of hidden treasure lies concealed. Never give it up, nor think that the days of making fortunes in the gold mines have passed; thousands will be making fortunes in the mines of California a hundred years hence. The mineral lands, as far as explored, are nearly four hundred miles in length, and from fifty to one hundred and fifty miles in width. This is a vast field for you to operate in; and if some of you have had bad luck for a time, do not despair, but let your watch-word be "work, wait and hope." If you have worked hard without realizing your desires, try again—try a new place—work, wait and hope, and your wishes will yet be gratified. In comparing the prospects of the miner of '48 with those of the miner of '52, the latter has a decided advantage over the former. It is true, in the old times we daily took out hundreds and thousands of dollars with a pick and knife; we made *piles* easy, and we spent it *tambien*,[1] for we expected it was to continue so forever. We had no means of enjoyment, not even a tent to cover us, and the provisions on which we subsisted were but sufficient to support life, and for which we paid high prices. You of '52 have to work hard and dig deep—you have every advantage of machinery and improvement to aid you, and your gains in many instances are nearly as large as in the olden time. Every comfort and luxury of life are at your command, and at prices that are reasonable; you are not *taxed* as we were then, yet you pay a heavy tax from your hard earnings. The tax here mentioned needs an explanation, to those who have never studied what it is. Since the day money first became an article of commerce, a swarm of Shylocks have been seen following the laboring man, and feeding and fatting off the sweat that labor wrings from the brow of the sons of toil. California has been a grand field for the operations of the pickers of human bones. To these—the buyers of gold dust, and the traders, who generally priced their goods so that their gains were regulated by the market value of gold dust—the laboring class have been paying a tax before unknown in the history of the world. In '48, when gold dust was worth but six dollars per ounce in coin in the mines, the miners paid to these plunderers two-thirds of their hard earnings. Shylocks in the coast towns gave eight dollars per ounce, thus taking from the miner five-ninths of his earnings, without giving him an equivalent. In '49, the average price of gold dust was about $14 per ounce, and two-ninths of the miner's hard earnings went to line the pockets of the eaters of human flesh. I make these calculations from the fact that the lowest assay of California gold at the U.S. mint has been over $18 per ounce; the difference between this, its lowest real value, and the prices the miners have received for it, is the silent *tax* which they have been paying. In '50 and '51 gold was worth $16 per ounce, leaving for the speculator one-ninth for his share. At present you only pay a tax of one-eighteenth of your earnings to the lordly speculator. In '48, if we made $500 per day, its value to the miner was but $200; if you make $600 at present, it is worth to you $566.66, your *silent tax* being only $33.33, instead of $400.

---

1. Spanish for *too* or *also*.

Disputed Claims

IF YOU REFUSED TO SELL OR SPEND YOUR DUST, and wished to send it to the mint, or any part of the States, you had, and have yet, to pay from five to ten per cent for that privilege. This *silent tax* has been paid into the pockets of speculators to the amount of full forty millions of dollars since the commencement of gold mining in California. This may be said to be the cause of the neglect of the General Government to furnish us with a mint, whereat the miner could have had the full value of his labor awarded him.

But this state of affairs is about to close. In a few months we fondly hope to have a mint of the U.S. in full operation here, that will close many a shop whose sign is, "*Se compra oro.*"[1] Getting the full value of your dust is not the only advantage the miner will derive from the establishment of a mint. A certificate or mint draft will cost you nothing to forward to any part of the world; you can send by this means from one hundred to one million of dollars to any point you desire, without having the *feeling* satisfaction of first paying from five to ten per cent for the privilege. Therefore, rejoice, *diggers*, for there are better and brighter days just ahead of you—"work, wait and hope."

Now, as regards miners' claims, and what we have to do to get along without shooting each other, and I will cease to annoy you with these letters.

During the years of '48, '49, and '50, the miners managed their claims in the different diggings quietly, and all went on smoothly. Different diggings, it is true, in many cases had different rules, and different amounts of ground to work on, but this scarcely ever caused any trouble. If disputes arose in regard to the ownership or

---

1. "Gold bought," or "We buy gold."

Benjamin Kelsey. (See pages 3 and 4.)

boundary of a claim, it was left to a decision of a few of the miners at work nearest to them, and such matters were quietly settled without cost to the parties. During 1851, many bloody affrays occurred in regard to disputed claims; the courts were frequently applied to, and in some cases their decisions have but made the difficulty worse. There can be no power to legislate for the government or apportionment of the public domain, but the Congress of the United States. President Fillmore, in his message to Congress, very properly recommended that the mineral lands of California remain *as they are*—a field in which the laboring man of every clime has a right to work without price or rent. The miners are thus left (and very properly, too,) to legislate for themselves, and make rules amongst themselves for the government of their claims.

It appears from the many disputes and law suits regarding claims in the mines, (especially in quartz veins, which will prove to be a source of profit for many years to come,) that the miners should make a uniform and established rule throughout the mineral region, setting forth what number of feet shall constitute a claim for each miner. For this purpose let delegates be chosen from each district— placer diggings, and for the different quartz veins;—let these delegates be *practical miners*—working men—not useless idlers or hangers on about the mines, who can be influenced by a few dollars; let a day be fixed for these representatives to meet in convention in some one of the most central mining towns, not at any of the cities away from the mines, where their deliberations could be influenced or disturbed by designing speculators or gas blowers. Let such a convention make rules for the government of mining operations, and make an uniform size to miners' claims in the different kinds of diggings, and let these be binding on all engaged in mining; in cases of

Ejecting the Squatters.

(Alonzo Delano, *Old Block's Sketch-Book.* Engraving by Charles Nahl.)

disputes or disagreements, let the disputants refer their case to a
board of arbitration composed of miners; let the decisions of these
boards be governed by evidence and the rules and regulations laid
down by the proposed convention; and then the rifle and knife, and
more than all, the *courts*, will be no more called into requisition for
the settlement of disputes. I am one who holds that the courts of
California, or of any other State of the Union, have no more right to
portion out or lay bounds to claims of miners in the mineral lands of
the U. States, than they have to portion out the flower gardens for
the Emperor of China.

The late miners' convention at Sacramento, has been of no benefit
to the miners. The whole mineral region should be represented in a
miners' convention, to be of any binding or lasting use; and such
resolutions as—a foreigner should not be allowed a like privilege to
work in the mines as an American, should have had an amendment
attached, such as: all foreign bankers, brokers, speculators and merchants, should not have the same privilege to swindle the miners out
of their hard earnings, as the American has. Such an amendment
would have at least made the wise resolution a little longer.

Another resolution of the miners' convention at Sacramento re-
commends a rail road from the Mississippi to the Pacific, to be immediately constructed. What a rail road has to do with the diggings,
would be hard indeed to tell. Such miners' conventions as have been
held so far, have rather tended to discourage the attempts of the
miners at forming a uniform mode for all mining operations than
otherwise. But try again, boys; send your delegates to a convention
from every portion of the mining region—men on whom you can
depend—and you may rest assured that the day will soon come when
you will have the means of settling any difficulties that may arise
amongst you.

These are the simple suggestions of an old miner, whose practice
and observations in the mines have prompted him to make. No doubt
they will be of but little weight with many but I hope they may be
read and thought of by the working portion of the mining community.
If, in these letters I have erred, it is human; if I have given offence
to any, I humbly beg pardon; if, on the other hand, they have proved
a source of interest or amusement to any, my task has been richly
compensated.

Tulare Plains

Climate, Soil, and Rivers

IN THE MANY HISTORIES AND SKETCHES which have been written on California, not one of them have given to the public any authentic account or satisfactory description of this vast body of valuable land, which has lain for ages the home of the wild beast of the field, where they have roamed in wild liberty over its vast and fertile bosom unchecked by the hand of man. The writer does not undertake this task for any other purpose than to give to the world a true and correct history of this valley, which remains a hidden mystery to even the nine-tenths of the inhabitants of California at the present day.

In extent this valley reaches from the head of Suisun Bay to Walker's Pass, within 120 miles of Los Angeles, being a distance of near three hundred miles in length. It is bounded west by the coast range of mountains, and on the east by the Sierra Nevada, and its average width is about sixty miles—measuring from the foot of the low hills on each side. The Moquelumne river may said to be the dividing line between the Tulare and Sacramento Valleys. This vast plain, containing 20,000 square miles of tillable land, and watered by many rivers, and beautified by lakes, is as yet an almost unknown portion of our State, as regards its value to the agriculturist and miner.

Its climate is, as Col. Fremont remarks, like that of Italy, although the middays of summer are, in many portions of it—especially the lower part of the valley—oppressively hot; yet the evenings and nights are deliciously cool and refreshing. From above the mouth of

the Merced to the head of the valley, a cool breeze blows from the
northwest from ten o'clock, A.M., until 10 P.M., which keeps the air
perfectly pure and refreshing throughout the summer months. In
winter, a perfect spring may be said to exist, as the centre of the
valley never is covered with frost or snow, except an unusual hard
winter prevails. Owing to the height of the upper part of the valley
above the sea, it makes the neighborhood of Buena Vista Lake one of
the most delightful and salubrious portions of California, and where
man has but to dwell for a season, and he becomes enraptured with
its loveliness.

Soil

The traveler, crossing this valley, or traversing it in any direction
during the dry season, would judge from its parched appearance
where it is not watered by the rivers, that it is a barren waste, unfit
for any purposes of man. This was the opinion I formed of it on my
first visit. Being a practical farmer, I had a curiosity to examine the
soil and the inducements offered by the general aspect of the country
to agricultural pursuits. The lower part of the valley consists of a
deep, rich, sandy loam, intermixed with stratas of decayed vegetable
matter, the whole resting on a bed of gravel or sand. The depth of
this soil varies from one to six feet, the deepest portions being near
the centre of the valley. The vicinity of the Tule Lake, and the large
body of land lying between the lake and the San Joaquin river consists of a like loam, intermixed with different species of clay. There is
no portion of this valley, from the head of the Tule Lake to Suisun
Bay, but is all that the agriculturist can desire, when aided by means
of irrigation. From the head of the Tule Lake to the vicinity of Kern
river and Buena Vista Lake, a distance of seventy-five miles, the valley may be pronounced a barren desert, with the exception of a strip
of some ten miles in width, bordering on the slough of Buena Vista
Lake. Around this lake and Kern river, the soil again assumes a rich
sandy loam. This barren portion of the valley is composed of red clay,
interspersed with different mineral substances, and so undermined
by gophers and kangaroo rats, as to be in many places impassable by
man or beast, even in the dry season. No live thing is to be seen upon

its dreary bosom, either animal or vegetable, with the exception above mentioned.

In the dry season there is not one drop of water to be found within the boundaries of its parched bosom. This relates to the valley only; in the coast range and Sierra Nevada, bordering on it, are to be found beautiful valleys, well timbered and watered. These valleys are formed by the long spurs making out from the mountains, and many of them offer every inducement to settlers, owing to their rich soil and unequalled climate.

Rivers

On the western side of the valley, from the Suisun Bay to the head of these plains, there is not one stream to be met with. During the rainy season, there are several small creeks running from the coast range into the valley, none of which continue to run only during the continuation of the rains. On the eastern side, in going south from the Moquelumne, the first stream met with is the Calaveras. This stream taking its rise but a short distance in the Sierra Nevada, is not affected by the melting snows, and is only a stream of note during the rainy season—during the rains, it becomes a deep and rapid river; its overflows form several of the sloughs in the vicinity of Stockton, but its principal body empties into the Moquelumne. From the middle of August to the first of November, it becomes dry, with the exception of pools found along its bed. All the springs and rivers of California commence rising some two or three weeks before the rainy season commences, and by the middle of November, the Calaveras becomes a running stream the greater portion of its length. It is useless for any purposes of navigation or for irrigating its valley.

The Stanislaus is a river of some note; taking its head far in the Sierra Nevada, it continues a large, deep, and rapid river from the first of December until the first of July, being fed by the rains during the winter, and the melting snows during the beginning of the dry season. This river could be made navigable for vessels of light draught, for 25 miles from its junction with the San Joaquin. During the dry seasons, its waters are sufficient to irrigate the entire plain lying between it and the Calaveras. The modes of irrigation from these rivers will be noticed in their proper place.

The Tuolumne is nearly the same size of the Stanislaus, and could be made navigable for nearly the same distance. It empties into the San Joaquin some ten miles above the mouth of the Stanislaus.

The Merced is a much larger stream than any yet mentioned, and could be made navigable to near the foot of the mountain during the season of high water. It empties into the San Joaquin some 25 miles above the Tuolumne.

The Mariposa, Chowchilla and Fresno rivers may be classed with the Calaveras, being running streams during the rainy season and spring only. These streams do not enter directly into the San Joaquin, but their united waters form the immense tule marsh between the bend of the San Joaquin and the mouth of the Merced; the water thus collected enters into the San Joaquin at many different points during high water. The Mariposa being celebrated for the rich mineral lands it drains, is formed by the union of Fremont's, Agua Frio creeks and their tributaries. After it enters the plains some five miles, it forks, and the water thus divided, continues its course towards the marsh, but the waters of them sink to such a degree, that the branches can be stepped across where they enter the tule marsh.

The San Joaquin is the next and last river that runs from the Sierra Nevada directly to the sea in this valley, and forms the main channel that drains the lakes and carries off the waters of all the rivers before mentioned. All the rivers that run into the tulare valley, having their heads in the Sierra Nevada, run into the plain, where they run nearly due west to the San Joaquin and the lakes. The San Joaquin is, with but one exception, the largest of these rivers. Where it leaves the mountain, it runs westward for upwards of forty miles from the low hills to the middle of the plains, where it suddenly bends to the N.N.W., and continues its course to Suisun bay. At its bend it is joined by the lake slough, which conveys into it the spare waters from the lakes in the plains above. The San Joaquin, for size and commercial purposes, may be rated as the third river on the western coast of America. By an outlay of some few thousand dollars in improving its navigation, by removal of points in the short bends and sand bars formed by them, vessels drawing two feet water could navigate it to within twenty miles of the point where it leaves the Sierra Nevada, during the year, a distance by the river of near four hundred miles. Vessels drawing from four to five feet water, can run up as far as the mouth of the lake slough during seven months in the year. As yet no inducements are offered to steamers to navigate the San Joaquin higher than Stockton, although they have been up as far as Graysonville;[1] schooners and brigs have also been up to this point. The writer has twice navigated this river, and once sounded it from Bonsell's Ferry[2] to the rapids at the foot of the mountains, and in regard to its capabilities for navigation, speaks from experience; but the obstructions above named must be removed to make it navigable as far as stated. The current of the San Joaquin is about 2½ miles per hour, from its junction with the lake slough to where it meets the influence of the tides.

King's river is nearly as large as the San Joaquin. It is navigable to the mountains, but its length from the low hills to where it enters the tulare lake, is only about 40 miles. It empties through several mouths into the northeast corner of the tulare lake, and is a beautiful and picturesque river.

---

1. Andrew J. Grayson, with two others, in April 1850 established a ferry and the town of Grayson City on the San Joaquin River, on the road from Pacheco Pass to Sonora—about eight miles above the mouth of the Tuolumne. There is still a small community named Grayson, about two miles northeast of Westley, on state route 33.
2. In 1848 Jacob Bonsell and John Doak started a small-boat ferry across the San Joaquin River about where the Southern Pacific Railroad and Interstate 5, between Tracy and Manteca, now cross. The place is presently known as Mossdale, after William T. Moss, the third owner of the ferry, who bought it in 1856.

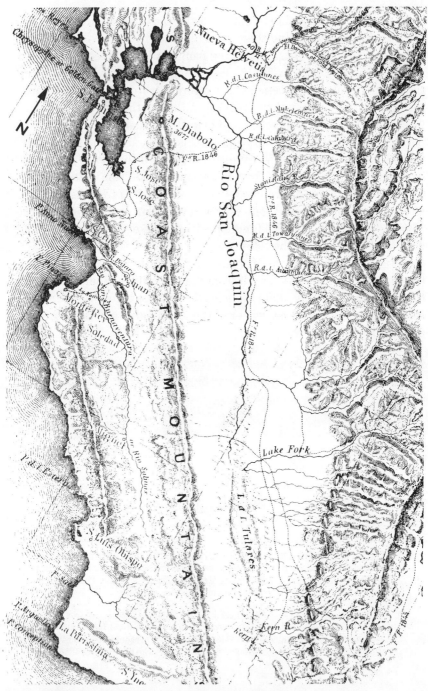

A portion of the *Map of Oregon and Upper California, from the Surveys of John Charles Frémont,* 1848. Drawn by Charles Preuss.

The Four Creeks, and the Lakes

THE FOUR CREEKS are the next waters met with. These deep and rapid streams are formed by one river. Lieut. G. H. Derby of the U.S. Topographical Engineers, who made the first surveys of this portion of California, in May, 1850, named this Francis [Frances] River. It is larger than the San Joaquin or any of its tributaries where it leaves the mountain.[1]

This stream can be heard when you have gone a few miles in among the Buttes at its entrance on the plain, thundering from the rocky heights of the sun-capped Nevada. Its waters, as if tired of their task, seem to stop to rest in a beautiful small lake, formed amongst the conical hills.

These hills divide the waters of Francis River at the foot of the Lake into the four streams known to the traveler on the plains as the Four Creeks. These Creeks meander thro' a heavily timbered and beautiful country, some 25 miles, where they empty their waters into the Tule Lake.

Allow me here to digress for a few moments from the tenor of these sketches, and you who admire the beauties of nature, untouched by the hands of man, accompany me to the top of the conical hill that raises its head near the mountain—far above the rest that surround it—and there view the fancy pencilings of the finger of the unseen Hand that formed from chaos this the most lovely spot in California. Now from its top we see around us a hundred conical hills rising from the plain, smooth and diagrametically shaped, as if done by the chisel of the artist. Here, too, the Sierra Nevada rises

---

1. The Kaweah River. It was discovered by the Gabriel Moraga expedition in 1806, and named *San Gabriel*. Derby did not name it *Frances River*, but simply noted the name on his map and in his report. He also described, but did not name, the Four Creeks. Including the main river, there were five distinct channels.

abruptly from the plains—its wall-like rugged sides running almost perpendicularly up, until its spiral peaks are capped with the eternal snows that shine with dazzling brightness from the rays of the rising sun. Yonder, far in the plain, rise tall spiral cones of long, slim rocks, whose bristling tops look like piles of spears stacked by giants of another age, who have long departed, and left their arms to turn to stone, beneath the petrifying hand of Time. Here, on the green plain, from where the Buttes rise, can be seen here and there the broad, low-spreading branches of the evergreen oak. The stillness of nature around is only broken by the thunder of the waters of Francis River as they come through the rocky gorges of the mountain passes; but, here at our feet, their white foam has died away, and in this crystal lake, where fish of a thousand species sport, they seem to stop and rest before they hurry on to their destination. Now, let us turn and look westward. The oaks, in their majesty, thickly cover the plain for miles around, and stretch away to the shore of the Tulare Lake. Amongst them and through high green grass, meander the Four Creeks. To the right, at the distance of 25 miles, runs the belt of timber, marking the course of Kings River to the lake. On the left is seen, at the distance of 20 miles, the broad body of timber that marks the course of Tule River. The body of land, thus bounded, is the best in the valley—well timbered and watered, and covered with the finest grass in California. Stretching beyond this to the west lie the placid blue waters of the Tulare Lake, whose ripples wash the foot of the low hills of the coast range—the blue tops of which sit a boundary to the scene.

As we look on this—the garden of California—the pride of an American heart makes our mind to people it with the hardy farmers of our country. We can imagine their neat cottages peeping out from amidst fields of flowing grain. We can see the neat village with its church spires, marking the march of civilization—and hear the lowing herds that browse on the luxuriant grass around. But those fancy pencilings of the mind are put to flight as our eyes fall on the scene at our feet. Here, at the foot of the mound on which we have been viewing the scene, the grass has been trampled down, the smoke of immense fires have scarce died away; the scene tells you that a large encampment has just left. Yes, it is the late camp of the Indian Commissioners. Those fires were their council fires, where they have been making treaties with the wild beasts of the field in human shape. Stand on the borders of this camp! a long line of ashes marks the place where once stood the buildings erected at an immense expence by the U.S.! there, too, almost within it, are twelve hillocks of fresh earth—they are the graves of twelve of our murdered countrymen! Here, over these smoking ruins—here, over the graves of our murdered companions have the soft hands of the Commissioners grasped in friendship those of the incendiary, and the murderers of our people. And, here, these good Commissioners signed away to the *Digger Indian* all the right of the white man to the best portion of this desirable spot. Can these treaties stand? Will the settlers in California submit to it? No! Look among the graves there! One looks greener than the rest! It is poor old Wood's grave! He was my old companion. We, together, explored the plains around, where the foot of the white man had never trod before. He was the first settler on the Four Creeks.[2] He now sleeps there, murdered by the Indians, who, instead of being punished, have been pampered, fed, and enriched by the *christian* hands of the Indian Commissioners.[3] But now the demon of Revenge has seized my soul, the blood runs boiling through my veins, the beautiful scene around has become dark and desolate. Come! let us hasten away, in our descriptive journey up the plains.

---

2. John Wood, who came to California in 1849, led a party that made the first attempt at permanent settlement in this vicinity. About December 1, 1850 the party located on the south bank of the Kaweah River about seven miles east of the present town of Visalia, and built a cabin. Shortly thereafter a band of Indians gave the whites ten days to leave that part of the country or be killed. The whites at first ignored the ultimatum, but then decided to leave—too late. The Indians attacked at exactly the end of ten days. Most of the whites were killed. Wood alone made it to the cabin; he was eventually captured, and skinned alive. The long-vanished town of Woodville was named for him.
3. Eighteen treaties were made throughout California between April 1851 and August 1852. Far from signing away the "right of the white man," the treaties actually stole the land from the Indians and left them with paltry reservations. The treaty referred to here may have been the one made at Camp Keyes on the Kaweah River on May 30, 1851. The treaties were a farce: the tribes of Indians were obliged to "hereby forever quit claim to the government of the United States to any and all lands to which they or either of them may ever have had any claim or title," (Robert F. Heizer, "Eighteen Unratified Treaties"). The Senate refused to ratify the treaties. They were filed under an injunction of secrecy, which was not removed until January 18, 1905.

The next stream above the Four Creeks, is Tule River, which is the last that enters directly into the lake. This river is near the size of the Tuolumne, and continues to run throughout the year. Five miles from this is Moore's Creek,[4] a pretty stream, which runs until about the middle of July. All the above mentioned rivers are well timbered with oak, and the valleys along them are everything that man can desire for the purpose of agriculture or grazing. The land lying between them only wants water to convert it into gardens.

From Moore's Creek to Kern River, a distance by a direct course up the plain of seventy-five miles, there is but one small stream running through into the plains, which is called Cotton Wood Creek,[5] in Lieut. Derby's survey. This stream ceases to run in July, but the thirsty traveler can find water in it any place in the low hills at any time of the year, by sinking holes a few feet in its sandy bottom. This creek is about halfway between Moore's creek and Kern river; the waters of this and Moore's creek, after forming a lagoon in the plains, find their way to the lake through a slough. A short distance from where the slough of Buena Vista Lake enters it, Kern river is the most southerly river of the Tulare Valley; it is a fine stream, and nearly as large as the San Joaquin. After running a short distance into the plain it branches out, and a large portion of it runs nearly northwest into the Lake slough; the balance of its waters are discharged into Buena Vista Lake. The whole or part of the waters of this river could, if necessary, be led along the foot of the low hills as far as Moore's creek, from which the plains now parched up could be irrigated. This, like the other rivers, is well timbered, and the land in its vicinity is of the most fertile quality.

Lakes

There are now but two lakes in the Tulare Valley of any note—the Tulare and Buena Vista. In Col. Fremont's survey the Tulare Lake is

---

4. Present-day Deer Creek, which heads in the mountains east of California Hot Springs, crosses highway 99 just north of Earlimart, and disappears into the sandy soil.
5. Poso Creek, probably the stream that Garcés called *Rio de Santiago* in 1776.

laid down as being double the size that it is at the present day; in 1842, when his survey was made, the body of water he has laid down did exist, but was two distinct lakes, divided by a high narrow ridge of land, and only connected by a slough. These lakes were known to settlers and priests of the missions of California; the lower one as *attache* and the upper one as non-*attache* lake. The *attache* now only exists, and is known as the Tulare Lake. It is about fifty miles in length by thirty in width; its length and breadth can be used for the purpose of navigation; its waters are now eight feet lower than they were ten years ago, and they continue yearly to decrease. It is fed by King's river, Four Creeks, Tule river, and the sloughs draining the upper water of the valley. The banks of the non-*attache* lake are still plainly visible.

The slough from Buena Vista Lake passes through its old bed, and during the season of high water, there are large lagoons formed in many places along in the bounds of the old lake.

Buena Vista Lake is a beautiful sheet of water, twenty miles long, and from five to ten in width; it lays nestled in the head of the valley, and is fed by Kern river and several small creeks which empty into it. The Sierra Nevada and coast range of mountains here unite, and form the head of the valley. The neighborhood of Kern river and Buena Vista Lake is such that the inducements offered to the settler will soon people it. The Cajon pass from Los Angeles, the Panoche pass[6] from San Luis, and the celebrated Walker's pass from the east, all come in here, in the vicinity of Buena Vista Lake. Colonel Fremont, in giving his opinion to a committee of gentlemen who had under consideration the great Whitney project of a railroad to the Pacific, informed them that Walker's pass was the only practical point for a railroad to be constructed through the mountains. Owing to Col. Fremont's thorough knowledge of the topography of these mountains, his statements can be relied upon; and if the iron horse ever snuffs the balmy air of California, it will be, as he imagines, from the hills at Buena Vista Lake.

The slough that conveys the water from Tulare Lake into the San Joaquin, is, during the high water, sufficiently deep to float vessels

6. Probably Pozo Summit.

of the largest class. Its length, from its entrance into the San
Joaquin to the edge of the tule beds of the lake, is about thirty-five
miles. Many are under the impression that this slough runs directly
into the Tulare Lake, and forms a navigable chain between the two.
That is not so. The depth of the slough is sufficient for any class vessel, but it is so crooked that it is difficult to sail through it in a small
boat; but the great preventative to its navigation is, that it does not
run into the lake.

The tules at the lower end of the lake are some fifteen miles in
width. The water of the lake oozes out through this for miles, and
then owing to the height of the lake above the slough, the water
begins to gather into small sloughs, and these, running to a common
centre, form, near the other edge of the tules, the Lake Slough.
Where the slough leaves the tules there is a fall of near five feet,
and the water runs rapidly for a distance of nearly a mile. The writer
made three attempts to enter the lake in a whale boat, but did not
succeed in getting over three miles into the tules, owing to the
slough spreading into hundreds of small branches, too narrow and
swift to get a boat through.

Lieut. Hamilton, of the U. S. Army, entered the lake from King's
river in a boat, and carefully examined the lower part of it, but could
not discover the least sign of any outlet to it. During high water
there is a slough which makes out of King's river, and running along
the edge of the tules of the lake, enters the Lake Slough near its
head. This slough could be navigated by small boats for about two
months in the year. The public may rest assured that there is no
direct outlet to the Tulare Lake, through which a boat can pass.

The slough connecting the Tulare and Buena Vista Lakes is about
eighty miles in length, and is navigable for small boats during the
greater part of the year. This slough passes through the bed of non-
attache lake, and during high water there is a lagoon forms on it,
near its centre, which is about twenty miles long and from one to
four miles in width. Travelers coming down the west side of the
valley, (which is by far the best route to the north or to the southern mines,) follow this slough, on which is good grass for animals
throughout the year.

Agricultural Resources

IN GIVING TO THE PUBLIC a description of the Tulare Valley and its resources, I am guided by personal observation, aided by the opinions of geologists, farmers, planters, and cultivators of the vine and tea tree, with whom I have had intercourse and consultation on the value of California as an agricultural country; or to what purposes its rich lands could be converted from the stillness in which they have laid through ages past, and made to swell our commerce and trade and enrich our people.

Six years ago the only knowledge that the world at large had of California, was by the topographical survey of Col. Fremont, whose reports started to our shores some of the hardy pioneers of the Western States. The accounts given by our naval officers, with but few exceptions, presented it as a barren country, unfit for anything but grazing purposes; yet all united in praise of its unequalled climate. The gold discoveries following the news of peace with Mexico, and the acquisition of California by the United States, had a tendency to retard the development of its agricultural resources for several years; but now its value, as such, is just being appreciated. Many now find that the potato and onion *diggins* fully equal in value any diggings yet discovered.

There is not one foot of California (the Sierra Nevada and gold region excepted,) on which wheat, barley and oats, cannot be raised to any extent desired. In the old States, as the farmer sows his seed, doubts cross his mind as to whether he will ever reap as much in quantity as he sows;—twenty-five fold is the greatest yield he can expect, and that on his best land, and all depending on the season.

But here the farmer can start at the mountain top and sow down to the depths of the valley, and *know* that the yield will be at least seventy-five fold. It is no rare occurrence here to reap from a hundred to a hundred and twenty-five *fanegas* to one sown; and in many instances three crops of barley and wheat have been raised from one sowing, the yield of the third year being half as good as the first. Under such circumstances, why should California yearly send millions of dollars to foreign ports for bread? It will not continue; the plough is about to work out a new state of affairs for us, and place California on an equal footing with her sister States;—we will soon have plenty and to spare.

I saw in 1850, a crop of barley raised on the Tulare Plains, equal to any I ever saw in the country. It was raised on a barren looking spot, where there was never any water except during the continuation of the rains. It was sown in December and gathered in June. The Tulare Plains will produce, without irrigation, small grain on every foot of them, with the exception already mentioned.

For the cultivation of corn and vegetables, irrigation becomes necessary; and for this purpose the great Unseen Hand has provided the waters that, with but a small exertion of the hand of man, will spread to any point he may desire.

The tule marshes, about which so much has been written, invite the planter to convert them into rice fields; they can be drained or flooded at pleasure for that purpose. Along the rivers and in the drained tule beds, hemp, flax and tobacco can be raised to an extent and perfection that would stand unparalleled. A gentleman from the southern states informed me that he had closely examined the soil of the Tulare valley, and that from his observations, he felt assured that cotton and the sugar cane could be brought to high perfection any place within the plain.

For the cultivation of the grape, California will contend with sunny France or Italy; and the whole of this valley could be made one vast vineyard and orchard.

We have amongst us several thousand of the inhabitants of China; a great many of them are intelligent men, from whom much reliable information can be obtained in regard to the introduction of the tea plant into California, and the value of our tule lands for the cultivation of rice. I have been assured by some of them that every inducement is offered for the introduction and cultivation of tea in California. These emigrants are, as a class, the best people we have amongst us—they are sober, quiet, industrious, and inoffensive. It is a rare occurrence that they appear in our courts, engaged in suits of any kind;

and never, under criminal charges, has one of them been tried, or one act of dishonesty detected amongst them. Those of them who understand the civil institutions of the United States, adore them; and on our festive days or days of celebration of our public achievements, the China men can be seen in great numbers in the ranks of our processions dressed in the grotesque costume of their country. Thousands of these men are ready to become citizens of the U.S., settle down, and turn our waste lands into beautiful fields, as soon as proper inducements and protection is afforded them; and no better class of men could be chosen to develop the agricultural resources of the Tulare valley than the Chinese who are amongst us.

Tobacco and flax now grow in a wild state on the middle portions of the tulare plains, and acres of it may be seen in different places around the lakes, and between the tulare lake and the San Joaquin.

The lands laying along the different rivers of the plains, are the most desirable of any in the valley; they can be successfully cultivated in any species of vegetation desired, without the aid if irrigation. Farms running two miles into the plains from those rivers, would be the most valuable of any in California. The soil is rich and deep, and the bottoms are heavily timbered with oak of the best quality, and sufficient for all purposes of fencing, etc. In cultivating the lands on the east side of the valley, between the rivers, an apparent obstacle may arise from the want of timber. This scarcity can be easily remedied, from the inexhaustible supplies of the finest timber from the adjacent Sierra Nevada mountain, not only for agricultural purposes, but for plank or railroads. If a railroad is ever constructed from the Mississippi to the Pacific ocean, it is most probable its course will be down the tulare valley, as Walker's Pass offers the only practicable point at which it can pass the mountain barriers that gird the Pacific coast. Every material for the construction of a railroad along the foot of the Sierra Nevada, is at hand the entire length of the tulare valley. It is but folly to doubt for a moment, in this fast age we live in, that a railroad will, at some early day, be constructed from the Atlantic States to California, connecting with an iron belt the two extremities of our Union. It is but for the American people to say it *shall be*, and presto, 'tis done. Things go too slow now between the two oceans to satisfy our fast propensities, and without some *genii* of the universal Yankee tribe should invent an ærial road, and some fine day come scanning it through the air, the railroad *will be built.*

The greatest difficulty under which the farmer labors in California, is the want of timber; but this is a small obstacle when surmounted by the introduction of wire fencing, which is as durable and efficient as that of wood. The rich lands that have been so successfully cultivated in the vicinity of the Mission of San Jose for the last two years, is at least twenty miles from any timber, but the deficiency is chiefly supplied by the wire fence. These fences can be put up at a less expense than those of timber, and are fully efficient in protecting crops against the depredations of stock.

Owing to the want of proper grasses ever being introduced on the tulare plains, it becomes bare during the dry season, with the exception of those parts watered by the rivers. On the lower side of the Stanislaus river, opposite Mr. Belcher's[1] ranch, a few Mormon families commenced a settlement in '47; they introduced there the red top grass, which is known as herd grass. This grass is the best that farmers can sow in the tulare valley; it forms a thick, substantial sod on marsh lands, grows luxuriantly on high and dry places; it affords excellent pasture during the year, and hay made from it equals the best cured clover hay. It can now be seen where it has spread from the Stanislaus to the French Camp above Stockton. The writer procured from this grass about a pint of seed in 1849, and scattered it in the bend of the San Joaquin where the earth was naked. It is now spread for five or six miles around, thickly covering the earth and affording the best of pasturage or land for cutting hay from. This grass is no doubt the best that can be introduced on the plains.

---

1. Belcher's name is on Gibbes' map of the San Joaquin River, 1850. It is on the south side of the river, opposite the site of the failed Mormon settlement of New Hope. Belcher established a ferry at that location in 1849.

Inducements and
Mineral Resources

THROUGH THE BARREN PORTION OF THE PLAIN between Moore's
creek and Kern river, there is a belt of land along the Buena Vista
Lake Slough, about fifteen miles in width, which could, by introducing on it the herd grass, be converted into the best grazing land in
the valley. Thousands of wild horses subsist on the grasses growing
there now. It is not the valley alone that can be made a garden of,
but in the coast range and Sierra Nevada, there are large and fertile
valleys, well timbered and watered, that will afford room for large
settlements. Nearly all the land on the rivers has already been taken
up by settlers, the Indian Reservations not excepted, as they are
generally the best in the valley; but a short time and squatters'
stakes will be seen planted all over the plains.

I would respectfully invite from our cities and towns the gentlemen organ grinders, cappers for gambling tables, runners for steamboats and hotels, venders of pies and parched corn, pickpockets, and
wharf loafers, who are now a nuisance to our communities, to take
a walk into the country and look at the rich lands that invite them
to honest labor and wealth. If you can make nothing by mining, the
farmer wants your services, for which he will pay you well. California is no place for you to follow your old callings; *it won't pay.*

The Tulare Valley is celebrated for being the most healthy portion
of California. The only place that is subject to disease of any kind, is
in the neighborhood of the Tulare Lake, where the ague is prevalent
at certain seasons of the year. Not only in the valley, but in the mineral regions bordering on it, prevailing diseases of no kind have as
yet made their appearance. The prevailing northwest winds during
the summer months, and the unparalleled purity of the air during

the winter in this region, warrants health, the greatest wealth man can possess.

The many inducements offered the agriculturist in this valley, and the many large and fruitful valleys adjoining it, in the coast range of mountains, must soon people it with a farming community. The rivers are highways to market, for all the produce raised in this section of country, and Stockton a market house for its reception. Every river of any note in these plains offer the best sites for mills or factories in California, as any water power desired can be obtained on them.

Mineral Resources

The mineral resources of the Tulare Plains, of themselves, is no doubt of but small importance; but the surrounding mountains are loaded with mineral riches, which are here included in the wealth and resources of these plains. All that portion of the gold region from Rio Seco, south, is included in what is known as the southern mines, and border on the Tulare Valley. These mines now receive their supplies through Stockton and the rivers above it. This region will be peopled with thousands of miners for a hundred years to come, who being consumers, will ever afford to the farmer a ready market for his produce, thus keeping within ourselves the wealth derived from our inexhaustible resources. Although millions of dollars have already been taken from the southern mines, their real value is but just beginning to be developed. The rivers draining this portion of the mineral lands of California, are not as rich as those of the northern mines, but the dry diggings, and the vast quartz veins, surpass in richness those of the north. The whole southern mineral region is traversed with the richest quartz veins ever discovered. Their number, richness, and magnitude, makes the word "inexhaustible" convey but a slight idea of their extent. Hundreds of square miles lying amongst these veins yet remain untouched by the miner's pick, although a rich deposit lies almost all over the region which they traverse—the depth, varying from the surface of the earth, where millions of dollars have been gathered, down to hundreds of feet. At Moquelumne Hill, Murphy's Diggings, and other places, many have realized large fortunes by sinking from fifty to a hundred and fifty feet in the hills, where at

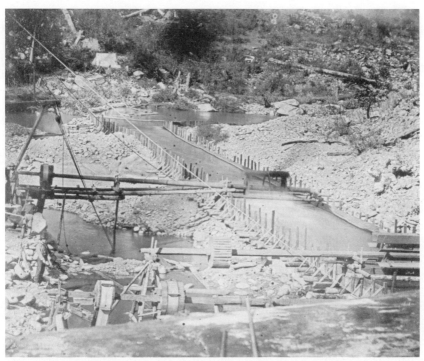

River mining at Grizzly Flats, El Dorado County, in 1850.

the bed rock the rich deposits are found;—and these places are but the beginning of what is to be realized in the mineral region by this source of mining.

There has been but little mining done south of the San Joaquin, but it is not because gold is not to be found there, both in placer diggings and quartz veins, that has prevented the progress of the miner south. The gold deposits between the Mariposa and Kern rivers are to be found far in the Sierra Nevada. The numerous veins of quartz bear to the south, and can be traced as far as man can get to the east in the Sierra Nevada. The writer has found gold on King's river, Tule river, and on a branch of Kern river, all of these places being far in the east. The mountains at the head of the valley become low, and can be passed with pack mules to the east at almost any point at the head of the Tulare Valley,—Walker's pass, however, is no doubt the best. The most correct map of the mountains at this, as yet almost unknown region of California, is the one made by the Jesuit Priest, in 1775.[1] A copy of these surveys, with an accompanying journal, is now in the possession of Dr. A. Randall,[2] of Monterey, a gentleman celebrated for his scientific acquirements, who is about to have the map and journal published. From this map it appears that these Priests here explored several hundred miles further up the Colorado than any surveys of the American government have been made, and traversed the region between the head of the Colorado and the head of the Tulare Valley, in four different directions. They describe the country as being broken by low ranges of mountains, interspersed with rich and fertile valleys; and, although the mineral resources of this section is untouched, yet it is evident that the belt of gold which traverses California passes into Sonora and Mexico through here.

Owing to the numerous tribes of hostile Indians, and the remote situation from supplies of the region south of the San Joaquin, but little has been done in mining operations, or any explorations of consequence made, and no doubt, from the appearance of this region of California, that gold deposits of unequalled richness lay yet untouched.

Silver, iron and cinnabar are also found in this region. In exploring in the neighborhood of Moore's creek, the writer, in company with others, found a shaft, partly filled up, that had been sunk apparently twelve or fifteen years ago; a part of the windlass apparatus was still standing, but in an advanced stage of decay. This shaft can be seen at the foot of one of the spurs of the Sierra Nevada, near Moore's creek, and about five miles from the edge of the plains. On enquiring of an Indian when and who had been at work there, he informed us that long ago some white men and Spaniards had been there, but they all died. This party were no doubt all murdered by the Indians. On mentioning this circumstance to Dr. A. S. Wright, a scientific gentleman

---

1. Probably a map made by Father Pedro Font in 1776 or soon thereafter, which shows the route taken in 1776 by Father Francisco Garcés from Mission San Gabriel to a point north of the Kern River. The map shows the Rio de San Felipe (Kern River), Rio de Santiago (probably Poso Creek), and the Santa Cruz (probably White River).
2. Apparently this is Andrew Randall, a gunner on the United States ship *Portsmouth*, in 1847. By 1850 he was referred to as a doctor and scientist, and later was a claimant of several ranchos.

for many years connected with many of the silver mines in Mexico, he informed me that from the description given, it was no doubt the same place worked by a company of explorers who were fitted out and went from Mexico to California some twelve years ago. He then informed me that in the archives at the city of Mexico, there was on record a letter from a Jesuit Priest, dated at one of the missions in 1776, informing the government that in the search amongst the mountains for sites for Missions, they had discovered silver in pure masses that weighed several tons; but to prevent a stable mining population from emigrating to California and destroying the prospects of the Missions, they had prohibited the Indians and others who accompanied them, on pain of excommunication and death, from disclosing where these deposits were. The knowledge of this record induced Mr. Wright and others of his associate miners in Mexico to fit out the exploring party before mentioned, which was put under the direction of a Mr. Hoyt. After several months absence, Mr. Hoyt sent to them from California some of the richest specimens of silver ore ever seen in Mexico; Mr. Wright described them as being almost solid silver. The place described by Mr. Hoyt, he informed me, agreed with the description given by me of the old shaft found on Moore's creek. After the receipt by them of Mr. Hoyt's letter and the specimens he sent, they never again had any tidings of himself or any of his party, although every inquiry had been made for him.

The coast range is known to be rich in silver and cinnabar deposits, but owing to the superior inducements offered in the gold regions, there is but little doing in them; but a broad hand points to a day not distant when the earth along these ranges will be disemboweled by the miner, and their now hidden riches be brought to light, to swell our wealth and fill to fullness the channels of commerce. I feel that I have but given an ungarnished, incomplete outline of the agricultural and mineral resources of the Tulare valley; but it is to be hoped that a geological survey may soon be made of the State, and those resources of it given authentically to the world. In the mean time, let writers remember that if they say anything against the resources of our State, they may rest assured they but expose their ignorance.

Charles M. Weber, founder of Stockton. (See page 4.)

Habits and Customs of the Indians

A S FAR AS THE EARTH HAS BEEN EXPLORED, man has been found inhabiting it, wherever it would afford him subsistence. Columbus discovered a new world—navigators after him discovered islands and continents—but on their landing, they met their own species in thousands, who were but little above the beasts of the field; but of all the human species yet discovered, none were ever found who approached so near the brute as the Digger Indian, found west of the Rocky Mountains in the U.S.

The Indians of the Tulare Valley number near 6,000; about one half of this number inhabit the mountains, and are fair specimens of the Digger race. The other portion inhabit the plains along the rivers and lakes—a great number of these are old Mission Indians— who have introduced many traits of civilization into their different tribes. The Notonotos[1] and the several different tribes of the Ataches,[2] are amongst those most advanced in many respects in the means of covering their nakedness and procuring a living such as human beings can subsist on. Those tribes that have intermixed with the miners in the different mining districts, have in a great measure laid aside their old modes of life, and to a great extent adopted that of the whites, at least so far as rascality extends.

Between the Digger Indians of the Sierra Nevada and the grizzly bear, there is but a slight difference existing, which amounts to the bear being brave, while the Digger is not. The Indian's superiority over the bear consists in his knowing how to talk and make fire;

1. The Nutunutu lived in the delta and slough area southwest of present-day Kingsburg, in the vicinity of Armona and Hanford. Their principal rancheria, Notonto, was on the north bank of the Kings River.
2. The Tachi, who inhabited a large area along the north and west shores of Tulare Lake, from the present town of Lemoore to Coalinga and close to the foothills.

Indians gathering seeds.
(Hutchings' California Scenes.)

otherwise they live on the same food, and their habits are similar. Between these two *animals* an eternal hostility exists. When the grizzly bear is aroused by the white man, if he is left to make his observations without being shot at, will, nine times out of ten, run away; but if an Indian and bruin come in contact, a foot race immediately takes place, as the bear invariably makes for the Indian with hostile intentions. If he succeeds in catching him, the consequence is, that there is a Digger less in a few moments; and many of those Indians are actually destroyed in this way. The cause of this hostile feeling between the two, I have often thought, is their great opposition in the acorn business. The habits and customs of the Digger Indian is that of no man in his most savage state. They have no article of covering for their bodies, but go naked as they came into the world from their birth, until the kind hand of death puts an end to their miserable existence. Their habitations, during the summer season, are constructed of the boughs of trees, placed in a circle in the ground, with their tops drawn together and formed into a cone of wicker-work. In these they reside until the frost of winter drives them into their *holes*, where they reside until the congenial suns of spring thaw them out again. These winter habitations are made by digging a circular hole in the earth, and placing over it a frame of poles, which is covered with bark or grass, over which the earth is piled to the depth of nearly two feet; an aperture is left in the side of this, just large enough to admit the body of a man, and serves as a door to the establishment. These huts are built without any regard to

regularity or uniformity in size. Each family has a separate one, and
they are made larger or smaller as the number of occupants require.
The captain of the tribe had his *hole* generally in the centre of the
rest, and is usually much larger than any that surrounds it. In looking into these habitations, the beholder, on first inspection, can
scarce believe that human beings could exist for a day under such circumstances; as they are unclothed—nearly unfed, and packed into
them in such small spaces as to prevent them from laying down, and
many of them hold continually ten or twelve, where there is not more
than room for three.

GOVERNMENT

To each tribe or rancheria, there is a captain or chief. Several
tribes are usually combined together by having a chief captain over
them, who holds despotic sway over his inferiors. The commands of
these captains are the law governing the whole. The right to rule
is hereditary in the male line, the oldest son taking the captaincy
occasioned by his father's death; but the rightful heirs are often
dethroned, and their places filled by the chief captain, by promoting
some of the tribe who have been successful in a thieving expedition.

RELIGION

As regards the knowledge of a Supreme Being, or the existence
of a soul here or hereafter, the digger Indian has not the least idea.
When questioned on this point, they reply with an empty, idiotic
laugh. They hold in high reverence any one possessed of the power
of doing things by the sleight of hand, or performing any feat of
which they have no knowledge. Necromancy is the only faith in which
they worship; and incantations and mysterious acts are universally
practiced amongst them.

Those tribes who are partially civilized by having numbers of old
Mission Indians amongst them, are but little superior to those in a
wild state, as regards religion or a knowledge of a Supreme Being.
The hold the priest as the power that alone can admit or refuse to
them eternal happiness. Since the demise of the old priests of the

different missions, they appear lost for consolation, but still believe that they are sure of eternal happiness, as they have been admitted into the Christian church.

MARRIAGES

When they want a squaw for a partner for life, (or rather for a slave,) the *hombre*, after watching those who are unmarried closely for a length of time, chooses the one who, in his opinion, is most expert in gathering roots and acorns, and can pack the greatest amount in her basket. After thus making his choice he asks the chief captain for her, who invariably gives his consent. When the fair one is informed by her lord that she is his lawful property for life, if she does not desire to become such, can refuse, but in her refusal she subjects herself to the penalty of becoming the common property of all the male portion of the tribe to which she belongs, and an outcast for the remainder of her life. Such a thing as courtship or love-making is unknown amongst them, but they are usually married young. Under these circumstances the inquisitive mind will ask, why are they not more numerous? why has not the digger race long ago overrun the Western world? These questions are easily answered. We must consider how many perish yearly from want and disease, owing to their mode of living and the inhuman articles on which they subsist; and, independent of this, after a man and woman have been *blessed* with a child, they do not cohabit or live together as man and wife until the child is some three or four years of age, and able to take care of itself. A natural instinct of man in his savage state prompts this mode of existence, where the means of subsistence are only gained by incessant application of the parents, even for themselves.

MODES OF BURIAL

The tribes who are under the constraint of the Mission Indians bury their squaws in a sitting posture; the men are, in most instances, burned, as with wild tribes, with the exception of those most civilized tribes around the lakes, who bury all their dead, and adorn their graves for a season with arrows, feathers, and all the fancy property of which they are possessed. Before the burial takes place the whole tribe spend a length of time in howling in piteous strains over the departed, who is finally consigned to mother earth, amidst incantations and presents from the survivors of his people.

Amongst the tribes of diggers in their natural state, their dead are invariably burned. This barbarous habit is dealt alike to man, woman and child, and is partly one of necessity, as well as usage, as they have no means of making graves for them; nor have they any tools of any description, not even a knife.

I have witnessed many of these funerals, of both sexes, from the aged, whose flesh had become dried and wrinkled by the length of years which he had trod the hills and vales of his nativity, down to the infant that had fallen from its mother's breast into the cold and sinewy hands of death. The first of these funerals which I witnessed was on the Cosumnes river, and the feelings of experience while reviewing it will never be erased from my memory. The rancheria to which the departed belonged, was a large one, situated in a beautiful bottom, from which arose tall pines, whose spreading tops formed a canopy above—around it arose high and rugged hills that gradually raised until their tops were capped by the everlasting snows, and

Indians burning their dead. (Hutchings' California Scenes.)

through it murmured the crystal waters of a fine creek. The scene
in all was beautiful.

On a cleared piece of ground, a short distance from the Buttes,
a vast heap of dry wood was piled, on which the departed was to be
laid and consumed. Curiosity led our party to the spot. The sun had
set, and night was drawing her sable mantle o'er earth, when the
whole tribe were chanting unearthly incantations around the fires
of their huts, until darkness had completely enveloped the scene.
Then arose a wild scream from out the hut of the departed that was
answered by every one in the camp—torches were lighted—and by
their glare the corpse was borne to the funeral pile. The body was
placed on the top of it, and more dry fuel heaped around. Then commenced the wild chaunt and incantations for the dead—fit music for
the funeral dance. The chief applied the first torch to the pile, and
in an instant it blazed forth in a hundred places. The screams of all
combined rose wild and unearthly. The forked flames that enveloped
the body shot high up amongst the tall pines, and lighted up the wild
spot around. When the body had become charred by the fire, poles
with sharpened points were repeatedly thrust through it, to aid the
flames in their work of destruction, and amidst the howlings of these
demons in human shape the death dance continued until the body was
consumed.

The funeral of a Captain is attended with more ceremony, and the
wailings are kept up for several days. The only marks of mourning
for the departed is worn by the squaws on the death of their husbands; it consists in daubing their foreheads, cheeks and breast, with
a mixture of pitch and coals from the funeral pile, beaten together.
During the time the squaw wears this mark of respect for the dead
her person is held sacred, and she is exempt from work of any kind.

Indian Modes of Subsistence

VARIABLE, DOUBTFUL, WONDERFUL, AND UNBELIEVABLE, are the ways in which the digger Indian supports life; he sows not, neither does he reap, but feeds upon grass and the roots of the earth, with the wild beasts; he knows no seed time nor harvest, but watches with a keen eye the growth of the grass and the fall of the acorn; he tilleth not the earth, nor buildeth stone-houses, nor granaries, nor lays up stores for the morrow, for fear they may spoil.

In the spring of the year the digger Indian lives on a species of clover, with which the small valleys in the mountains are covered, from the first of April until the drought of the summer months dry it up. The grass is fine, soft, and sufficiently nutritious to support human life, with some few roots gathered by the squaws from the creek bottoms. When this grass is no longer fit for use, the seeds of different species of weeds, young shoots of tule, bugs, worms, frogs, snakes, and many kinds of small roots, are the food of these beings until the low stages of water in the rivers. The rivers are filled with the finest fish in the world, and when the water is low they are enabled to catch with their

Indians grinding acorns.
(Hutchings' California Scenes.)

hands, spear, and shoot with arrows, any quantity of them they may desire. During this time they feast daily, and become, in some instances, almost torpid. The fall of the acorn is hailed as a jubilee, and at the season when fish and acorns are very abundant, they hold their annual feast, which usually continues for several days. At these feasts, if a horse or bullock can be obtained, by stealth or otherwise, it is barbecued in a way peculiarly *digger.*

During the winter months, when the rains have rotted the seeds, and the acorns have been consumed, a few roots, the seeds of the bur of the white pine, and such insects and small animals as they can kill, constitute their entire means of subsistence. Many must annually die from starvation, as they make no provision for the winter season. Some few tribes, where the Mission Indians are mixed with them, lay up quantities of acorns by making frames of twigs in the forks of the trees, out of the reach of the grizzly bear, which are used in the winter season.

The labor of procuring this subsistence, precarious as it is, is performed by the squaws. They labor incessantly from day light until dark, while their lords and masters lie around their camps from one day to another in perfect idleness, and apparently happy amidst their misery. They have no thought of to-morrow, nor care about futurity.

TRADITIONS OF THE NOTONOTOS

As I remarked before, the Notonotos and Ataches, having ascertained that the government of California had passed into the hands of the Americans, hastened to make treaties with Col. Mason, Military Governor of this State, at that time. The stipulations of these treaties only bound them to respect the American flag and people, and to be at peace with the whites, for which the American arms were to give them protection. No broad and fertile lands were asked for or given.

These Indians inhabit the shores of the lakes north of King's river, and cultivate corn and vegetables. They also catch and dry fish, kill wild horses and jerk their flesh, and generally have plenty to eat. A great portion of them go to the settlements and towns during the summer and work, for which they get well paid; they then purchase blankets and clothing, and but few of them go naked in the winter season. Their habitations, also, approach more towards civilization, being made of mats or woven tule and flags, which are stretched on poles similar to the lodges of our Eastern Indians. Their lodges also contain many of these mats, on which they sleep.

I have been several times at their rancheria, and partaken of the hospitalities of the Notonotos. It is situated on a point of land formed by the junction of King's river with the Tule Lake. These Indians are intelligent, hospitable, and great friends of the white man; and the only Indians in California, perhaps, that have anything like traditions or recollections of the past history of their race or country. They keep also a species of reckoning of time, by cutting notches in a stick.

This log or history is kept by old men, who appear to have the highest respect paid them by their tribe. Each notch in their stick has a legend or traditionary tale of the times in which it was made. I would recommend those in search of antiquarian knowledge to pay the Notonotos a visit, especially if they are prepared to undergo an age of deep study in deciphering back over these curious Indian records. From all the explanations they could make to us concerning the length of years, or a translation of their time into that used by Christians, we could make no comparison, although every exertion was used.

They have no numerals to express a greater number than ten, which is a great detriment in finding out any time kept by them. Amongst the many legends which they entertain is one which bears with it some shade of probability, as it points to a phenomenon in na-ture that we can see as being possible: They say that many moons ago their tribe were large and powerful men; that in those days all the great valleys of the Sacramento, San Joaquin and Santa Clara were one sea, that had no outlet where it now has at San Francisco, and the waters of it rushed into the sea near Monterey through where Pajaro river now runs; but when their people were great and powerful the mountains melted and burned up, and in the flames their people were almost destroyed, and while the mountains con-tinued to burn, the earth shook and the great hills fell down, and the water rushed over them into the sea where they now do, at San Francisco, and left these valleys dry. This tradition is also related by the remnant that is left of the Santa Cruz Indians; and from the formation of the country to which it relates, it bears a likelihood to truth. On the Tulare Plains there is to be found pieces of shells and fossil remains. These shells, in many instances, are found in the low hills 70 feet above the level of the plain imbedded in strata of sand stone and gravel. The formation of the earth in the valley and low hills is in all a great field for the attention and research of the geologist.

I have no doubt lengthened the description of the Indians of the Tulares to a tiresome point. The traveler on the plains will find them as presented. But watch all of them, for treachery is one of the prominent features of their character; and when their numbers in the mountains will justify them in an attack on the traveller, they will avail themselves of every opportunity where there is a prospect of success, and no fear of detection deters them.

An Indian fandango. (Hutchings' California Scenes.)

Wild Horses

Of ALL THE DUMB CREATURES that have been created for the use of man, the horse stands the most noble and useful. To see the horse in all his beauty, you must view him as he prances on the wide and wild plains of his nativity, unbridled or unchecked by the hand of man.

The Tulare Valley, perhaps, contains a larger portion of wild horses than any other part of the world of the same extent. On the western side of the San Joaquin, they are to be seen in bands of from two hundred to two thousand. These bands are to be met with at intervals from Mount Diablo to the Tulare Lake. The traveller, in going from the mouth of the lake slough to the head of the lake—four days travel—can see the plains covered with these fine animals as far as the eye can reach, in every direction. There are but few horses on the eastern side of the plains, with the exception of that portion lying between the San Joaquin and King's Rivers, and running down to the lake slough, where there are a great number yearly taken in this range by the Spaniards at the point called Ponts [Puente] de San Juan. These animals are never seen in poor or thin condition; a circumstance that of itself speaks volumes for the value of the country they range over for grazing purposes. Besides the innumerable quantity of these noble animals that are to be found on the plain, the large and fine valleys in the coast range have also their quotients.

The wild horse of the Tulares ranks amongst the finest of his species. He, unlike the common mustang to be found in southern portions of America, is of fine size, unparalleled proportions, and as fleet as the wild winds he breathes. They are of every color, from a glossy black to pure white. When these animals are caught, they are soon tamed, and can endure any amount of hardship without any other sustenance than the pasturage that the country affords. The Spaniards frequently travel on one of them from seventy-five to one hundred miles per day. For endurance of fatigue on pasturage alone as subsistence, the horses of California have no equals. The writer, in 1847, took two horses from the U. S. cavalada [caballada] at Monterey, (from the pasture) and rode them, alternately, on an express, one hundred and forty miles in ten hours and forty minutes, a feat that the officers who were in Col. Mason's staff at the time, well remember. The same horses were in use the following day, with no appearance of stiffness or marks of fatigue.

Amongst the wild horses on the Tulares, many are apt to be seen with the brands of the Missions and ranches on them; and to what age these animals will remain serviceable, or how long they live, cannot be ascertained, as no notice has been taken of their longevity; owing to their spirit and breed, the word "old horse" is scarcely ever applied to one of them, although many are known to be over twenty years of age.

Amongst those animals that have escaped from their captors and are enjoying sweet liberty on the rude and grassy plains of the Tulares, is that famous horse Sacramento, raised by Capt. Sutter. This horse has been frequently seen by Spaniards (who know him well) while running horses on the plains. As Sacramento's history is a singular one, I must be allowed to digress until I give a brief sketch of it. He was raised by Capt. Sutter, on the Sacramento, is a fine large iron-grey, and fate apparently destined him to figure in the past progress. He was presented to Col. Fremont, by Captain Sutter, as part of his fit out on his return to the United States, from his first tour of exploration to California; he was the pride of that expedition. He was taken to Kentucky, where he was a universal favorite and pet, and being a stranger from California, he was also looked upon as a curiosity; but destiny had marked him out for his course, and he was doomed to leave the quiet retreats and shelter of civilization, and tread again the boundless, trackless wilderness between there and the Pacific. He arrived in California again in time to be of considerable service to the patriots of the Bear Flag army. He was sent from Sonoma to Monterey for the service of Colonel Fremont's battalion. On the way down the party in charge of the animals for the battalion, twenty-seven in number, were attacked on the Salina Plains by one hundred and fifty Californians, when the short and bloody fight of the Salina was fought, and the Spaniards put to flight. Sacramento, in this battle, was ridden by the lamented Capt.

Burroughs. Partaking of the impetuous fire of his rider, he plunged
into the ranks of the enemy; there he pranced with the gallant
Captain, who continued to deal death around him until he fell.
Sacramento did not apparently feel the loss of his rider, as he was
still seen prancing amongst the enemy. The uneven struggle was
short and the Californians were defeated.[1] Their retreat was wild,
rapid, and disorderly, and in the midst of their flying squadrons,
Sacramento could be seen with head and tail erect, apparently glory-
ing in their defeat; but he soon found that he had lost his rider and
his own cavallada, and left the enemy's ranks and returned with a
loud exulting neigh to the American camp. He was next ridden by
one of Col. Fremont's officers on the campaign to the Southern part
of California, until the treaty of Los Angeles released him from
military service. He was afterwards sent to a ranch, with a view of
giving him some rest; he had remained but a short time in retire-
ment, however, before a band of thieving Indians from the Tulares
visited the settlements and stole him with many other horses, and
made for their haunts in the mountains, with the intention of making
a feast upon the flesh of our noble animal. But Sacramento, as if conscious of his fate, and feeling himself deserted by the Americans,
whom he had so faithfully served, determined to declare his independence of the human family, and carried out his resolve by making
good his escape from his captors, and joined one of the vast herds of
his species that inhale for ever the free winds of the valley. In this he
showed a spirit imbibed from those he had served. He is now wild
and free, and amidst the whirling herds can be seen his noble proportions, which freedom has developed to fulness; but apparently knowing the hardships to be endured in bondage, he only comes near
enough to the hunters to see that they are men, and then flies as the
wind, aided as he is by fear of the unerring lasso, until distance hides
the hated objects from his sight. Keep clear, brave horse, for well you
know your fate if you are again caught in the toils. You have seen
man long enough to know him; you know the voice that was once kind

---

1. The Battle of Natividad, which took place November 16, 1846. The Americans
   had four killed and four wounded; the Californians had somewhat greater losses.
   The site is about seven miles northeast of Salinas.

to you has often bid you to go, in harsh, unmeaning tones; the hand
that caressed you also placed within your mouth the iron bit and
guided you a beast of burden through rough and thorny ways, on
desert lands and mountains wild; you proudly bore the warrior to the
fatal charge upon the battle field, where you learned that man oft
sought the life of his brother for nought but power, and to bow the
neck of the one to the other, as the fate of the contest might decree;
and you would have soon been converted into food for him if he had
needed you for that purpose; you have lived too long amongst the
free, not to dread again the yoke of bondage.

MODES OF CATCHING HORSES ON THE PLAINS

The greatest number of horses are taken by making strong cor-
rals, and running the bands into them. The hunters first ascertain the
range of a band, and then select a suitable place to build their corral,
which is done by making a pen of heavy timber, to which is left a narrow opening. On the outside, leading from the gate are built wings
which gradually widen out for a long distance. When this is completed the band are surrounded by the hunters and driven in, where they
are lassoed and tied together.

But there are great numbers taken with the lasso. For catching
horses in this way, the best and most fleet horses that the rancheros
possess are selected, and are not used for several months before
the running season, which is usually in the months of May and June.
Then they go into the plains in the vicinity of the most numerous
bands, and make their encampment and corral. When they get prepared for running the bands, a scene of wild and glorious excitement
commences, which must be seen to be appreciated.

There are no people in the world that can surpass the Californians
in horsemanship. In the use of the lasso—that indispensable appendage to a Californian's outfit—their dexterity cannot be excelled.
They will catch an animal, while at full run, around the neck or by
either foot they may desire. The unerring precision with which they
throw the lasso is only attained by long practice. In catching wild
horses, the runners usually number from ten to fifteen. In preparing for the chase they put nothing on the horses they ride with the

Lassoing wild horses. (Vischer's *Pictorial of California*.)

exception of a light bridle or halter, and a strong belt around the body of the horse, to which the end of the lasso is fastened. As soon as the band of wild animals make their appearance, the runners mount and remain on their horses until the band come to a halt. The wild horses, when they see any strangers in their vicinity, make a rush in a body towards them, and when within forty or fifty yards make a halt, and if nothing frightens them they will come close up. It is at this indecisive halt that the hunters partake of the first wild feeling of delight, which is ever attendant on the sports of the chase. If the hunters are unobserved by the band, they soon intermix with the animals on which these men are mounted, and become an easy prey to them, each one of whom never fail to catch one. But if the band becomes frightened and start off from them, then commences a scene of rare and glorious sport. The wild band of animals, the hunters, and the horses upon which they are mounted, all seem to become possessed of a glorious monomania, which propels them over the level unbounded plain faster than the hurricane's wild winds.

As soon as the animal caught has been choked down by the tightening noose, which is usually but a few moments, the horseman dismounts and shifts his bridle and girth to the captured horse, and mounts him and teaches him to be the servant of man from the hour of his capture.

The increase of the wild horses of this country is very slow. Besides the large numbers which are annually captured, there are bands of wolves and cayotes continually hanging around the horses, feeding on the helpless colts, few of which escape until they become large enough to defend themselves.

ANIMALS AND GAME

Every beast and bird of the chase and hunt are to be found in abundance on the Tulares. Horses, cattle, elk, antelope, black tail and red deer, grizzly and brown bear, black and grey wolves, cayotes, ocelets, California lions, wild cats, beaver, otter, minks, weasels, ferrets, hare, rabbits, grey and red foxes, grey and ground squirrels, kangaroo rats, badgers, skunks, musk rats, hedge hogs, and many species of small animals not here mentioned; swan, geese, brant, and over twenty different description of ducks also cover the plains and waters in countless myriads, from the first of October until the first of April, besides millions of grocus (sand hill crane,) plover, snipe and quail. The rivers are filled with fish of the largest and most delicious varieties, and the sportsman and epicurean can find on the Tulares every thing their hearts can desire. Parties of gentlemen from our cities, who wish to leave for a time the confines of their narrow limits of business, and enjoy the exhilarating pleasures of a trip into the interior, can find their every wish gratified by a journey up the Tulare Plains. April and October are the best seasons—April in particular—for at this time game of every description is most abundant, and the plains and mountains are one continued bed of roses and gaudy flowers; even to breathe the air is life and health itself. Go up by land as far as the lake, and return by water, and you will ever bless the time you made the excursion. The western side of the plain is the best travelling, and the range of the greater portion of game. In such an excursion you can unite business with pleasure, as you can see and judge personally of the value of the Tulares for agriculture, and her noble river for the purpose of navigation.

The Bright Gem
of the Western Seas

Reclamation of the Tule Lands

THIS MATTER HAS BEEN so often and ably discussed, that to say much more on the subject would be but a repetition.

The Surveyor General, in his last able report, estimates the swamp lands of the State at 2,622,400 acres. This estimate will be found upon actual survey to be over large, but it is the only authentic calculation now before us. As I have undertaken to give a brief, but *reliable* sketch of the Tulares, of which these swamp lands form a large portion, the public must permit a lengthy review of this subject, which at present absorbs so much of the public attention.

By an act of Congress, approved Sept. 28th, 1850, all the swamp or overflowed lands in California were donated to the State; provided that the proceeds of said lands, whether from sale or by direct appropriation in kind, shall be applied *exclusively*, as far as necessary, to the purpose of reclaiming said lands by the means of levees and drains.

Besides this, we may rest assured that as liberal grants of land will be made to the State for the purpose of education, as have ever been made to any of our new States. These, with the addition of the mineral lands, should satisfy the land-craving appetites of our people. I do not belong to the "vote yourself a farm" party, but hope to see the General Government receive payment for the remainder of her lands in California, as she has done in all other States. The *give away* system of the public domain, advocated by so many, would but tend to retard the progress and settlement of the State, as numbers would accept the gift for the sole purpose of speculation; while those who wish to become permanent settlers and improve the public lands, would in nine cases out of ten prefer paying the government price for it, and receive their titles from the U. S. for *value received*.

From present appearances settlers can have no hope of receiving a *free* farm from the State government, out of lands granted it. There was an act of the State Legislature, passed May 1st, 1851, granting to all persons settling on the school lands prior to the 1st of January, 1852, privilege to hold the same, on *payment of three dollars per acre into the treasury*, consequently a free farm cannot well be expected out of the school lands. This is but one of the many acts of California legislation, which has been considered in weakness, engendered in water, and brought into existence through a womb of wind.

Our present Legislature is looking a little further ahead than the last, and have *appropriated* the proceeds of the sales of public lands for the sinking fund of the State debt. They certainly cannot mean the funds created by the accumulation in the treasury of those three dollars per acre for the school lands. No! it must be the tule lands which they expect to realize a *pile* from. They have overlooked the *proviso*, our old Uncle made, in his generous donation—to "first reclaim these lands," by donation or by applying the funds realized from their sale to that purpose. There cannot be many of our law-givers who have ever taken interest enough in the well-fare of the state, to take a correct view of the swamp lands in the Sacramento and Tulare Valleys, or those of other portions of the state and thereto estimate the cost and labor of reclaiming them. If they had, they would have went to the Legislature fully prepared, to "vote a farm" out of them, instead of making wild and boundless calculations of the immense sums that are to be realized to the state from their sale.

But to return to the modes of drainage of *swamp lands*, in the Tulare valley. The *tule* or swamp lands, on the San Joaquin, above Stockton, are principally formed by the sloughs making out of the river, and not caused by general overflow, as many suppose. The greatest distance of the overflow of the San Joaquin is not over one-half mile, and there are but three or four places of this kind, to be met with between Bonsell's Ferry and the head waters of the San Joaquin. To convert the present tule marshes into fruitful fields, it is but necessary to build levees at these places, and at the low stages of the river, to fill up the mouths of the sloughs, that lead out into the plain. The largest of the sloughs of the San Joaquin, is the San Juan, which forms a short distance below the mouth of the Lake Slough, and meanders through the plain until it enters the river again opposite the mouth of the Merced, being a distance of near fifty miles. In many places it approaches within eight or ten miles of the foot of the Coast Range. There are many small sloughs, that cross from the river and enter into the San Juan. The over-plus of all of these, form the marshes met with in the fine body of land laying between the river and slough. The land thus watered is of the best quality, and situated as it is, mid-way of the valley, it enjoys a climate that may be pronounced a perpetual spring. On the eastern side of the river and of nearly the same length, is the immense tule swamp formed by the waters of the Mariposa, Chowchilla and Fresno rivers. This swamp is from one to ten miles in width, and is of equal value as that on the opposite side of the river. The bottom of this marsh is as low as the bed of the San Joaquin, and the waters collected in it from the three rivers, above mentioned, enters the San Joaquin promiscuously along the whole length of the marsh—after its bed becomes filled sufficient to overflow. To reclaim these swamps it would be necessary to cut and construct by levees, channels for the three rivers into the San Joaquin, it could then be kept drained or flooded at pleasure, during the year.

The marsh formed on the west side of the river by the San Juan, can be reclaimed by the stoppage of the mouths of the sloughs which create it. The modes of drainage of these two principal marshes, can also be used for the purpose of irrigation, by floodgates at the different embankments. All the marshes on the west side of the river, down to Martinez, and on the east side as far as Bonsell's ferry, can be drained in like manner as those above mentioned.

The immense marsh between the San Joaquin and Sacramento, containing many hundred thousand acres, can *all* be reclaimed by levees and drainage. The soil in the tule marshes is of inexhaustible fertility, as it is formed of decayed vegetable matter, of several feet in depth, and the soil and climate admirably adapted to the production of sugar cane, rice, cotton, hemp, flax, tobacco and all the grains and vegetables known to agriculture.

It is an easy matter to set down and detail these modes of reclaiming the tule lands, but when it is properly considered, it becomes

apparent that immense capital, or the united labor of large numbers
of settlers can alone accomplish this desired object. These lands must
be reclaimed by donation or the proceeds from the sales of them,
before they can be legally granted by the State of California. If they
are to be reclaimed by putting them up and selling them to the highest bidder, for the purpose of applying the amount thus obtained in
their reclamation, then it is obvious that they will forever remain
tule marshes, for the amount they would bring would not reclaim
scarce a thousand acres of them.

The only benefit the State can ever expect to derive from these
lands, is to get them under cultivation as soon as possible. Let the
State grant them, gratuitously, to individuals, associations or companies, in small or large bodies, or any way they can, so as to bring
them into use by being drained and cultivated; withhold from the
grantees the power to sell or convey away their tracts until they
had cultivated them successfully, two years in a reclaimed state,
so as to prevent a re-sale or system of speculation in them.

Under present circumstances, these lands are of no earthly use
to the State, nor will they ever be otherwise except by gratuitous
grants. There are capitalists and private individuals ready now to
reclaim these lands, under this system. The increase of the State
revenues from the taxation on the improvements and increased
wealth on these lands, would amount in five years to a greater sum
than they can ever be sold for, and at the same time permanently
attach to our soil thousands of a wealth-producing population, who
will otherwise necessarily be compelled to seek a home elsewhere.

MEANS OF IRRIGATION

The foundation and waters for irrigating the Tulare Valley, have
been furnished by the Allwise Creator, that man in due time might
apply them to fertilize the rich earth with moisture that is not
blessed with the "rains of Heaven in seed-time and in the time of
the ripening fruit." The plains have a gradual descent from Buena
Vista lake to the bay, and from the foot of the mountains on each
side to its centre. To irrigate the eastern portion, it is but necessary
to construct dams at the foot of the low hills on the different rivers,

and lead the water through channels to any portion of the plain desired. The fall of the land is sufficient for this purpose, and not so great as to cause a waste at the sides of drains by a too rapid descent. The land is superior in quality and better adapted to the purpose of irrigation from the rivers, than the Salt Lake Valley, where the Mormons have so successfully converted the waste and parched wilderness, by irrigation, into fruitful fields. The land lying between Tule and King's rivers can be cultivated in any way desired without the means of irrigation, although the means are at hand, if required, from the Four Creeks or either of the rivers. Between King's river and the San Joaquin, the land is now watered by the numerous sloughs which make out from these rivers, and meander in every direction through the plain between them during high water, which is in June and part of July; the very season their fertilizing influences are required. All the rivers of the plain can be divided into as many different channels as may become necessary for the purpose of watering the spaces between the upper streams, by diverting the water out of them at the foot of the low hills. It cannot be expected that the State or General Government will ever construct means of irrigation for any portion of California; and it must necessarily be done by the settlers on them. There are at present nearly enough of settlers on the Calaveras, Stanislaus, and the lands lying between, to make it profitable to them to divert the waters of the Stanislaus into the plain occupied, for the purpose of irrigation, which will no doubt be done within the next three years. If farming is done properly, the waters of the rivers will be required for its aid during the time they are swollen from the melting snows in the mountains, in the months of May, June, and beginning of July, and an abundant supply can be easily obtained.

The western side of the valley is dependent on the San Joaquin alone for its means of irrigation. The sloughs that now make out from it, can be used for the purpose desired. The San Juan slough can be led to the foot of the low hills, from where it now makes out, and thence down the whole length of the valley, from which all the land between the other sloughs and marshes can be watered.

As I before mentioned, irrigation is unnecessary for the cultivation of small grain in any part of California. The luxuriant growth of wild oats that are to be seen from the valleys to the highest portions

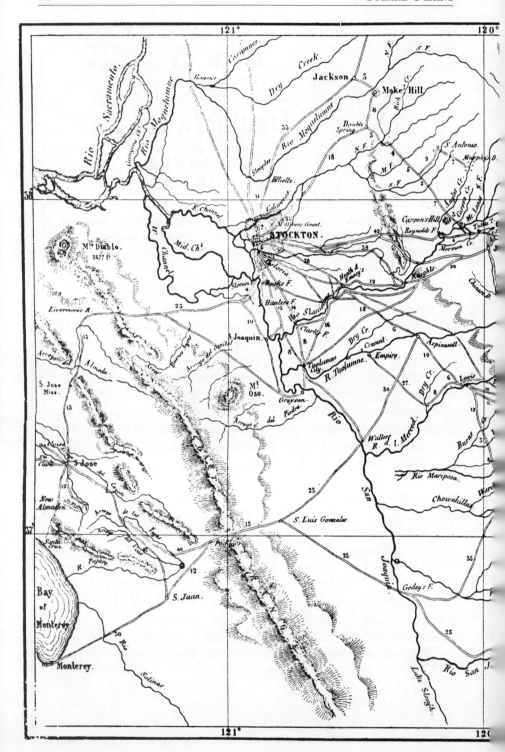

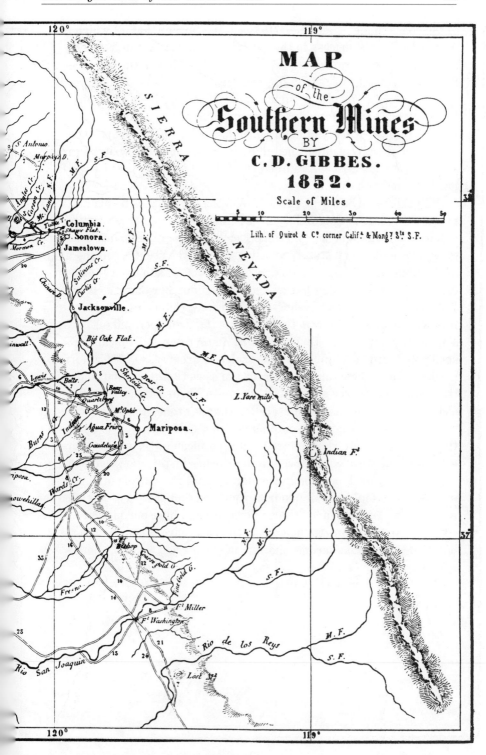

MAP

of the

Southern Mines

BY

C. D. GIBBES.

1852.

Scale of Miles

Lith. of Quirot & C?. corner Calif? & Mong? S?. S.F.

of the coast range, is sufficient to teach the farmer that all which is necessary for his success in the cultivation of small grain, is to sow it so that the first rains may bring it up, and he has nothing to dread from the drought of the long dry seasons.

The descriptions of the Tulare Valley that have been given in these letters to the Republican, are but faint outlines of the true worth of this vast body of land, which has been so long overlooked. To attract the attention of the public to it, has been the writer's great aim; but go and see it for yourselves, and you will find that its worth has but half been told.

Will this valley ever be settled? Will the bare places be made green with fruitful fields, through which the diverted crystal waters will be seen winding their fertilizing courses? Will the farmer's cottage, or the planter's stately mansion enliven the scene? Will the hum of the flouring mill and the factory's roar, ever waken from the sleep of ages the stillness that has ever reigned along her mighty rivers? Will the whistle of the fire-horse, as he comes thundering on his iron way, ever startle from their coverts the wild deer and elk? The answer is yes! and that, too, at no distant day, will all this be seen and heard. The unmeasured strides to greatness that California has been and is now taking, warrant the assertion. The thousands of the young and hearty sons of toil whom we see around us that have come to make this their homes, tell in thunder tones that with the blessings of God, that here nothing is impossible—that here, under the blessings of our glorious free and republican government, there has been a new era commenced in the world's history, so great that the civilized world looks on in wonder. Let not the wheels of government become foul and fall in our way, or obstruct the paths in which we are now treading, and "the wilderness shall blossom as the rose," our mighty mountains tunneled, our thousand rivers confined to their beds, and California become the seat of commerce, wealth, science and art,—

The bright gem of the western seas.

Life in California

The Latest News

How OFTEN DO WE MEET with the above caption in the eastern papers, and a half column or more under it with a detail of some horrid murder, or the proceedings of one of our lynch courts. If those who write from California for the papers in the eastern States, would detail life as it is here, even if they did sprinkle some of the horrible with it, the probability is that the quiet, religious, "old folk to hum" would not have their nerves so often disturbed, or be made to pronounce us so frequently as a "horrid set," and poor unoffending California as a "wonderful wicked" country.

We can imagine ourselves looking in on one of our good old, quiet family circles in lands "far awa'," when the old hearth stone has all the inmates gathered around it, listening to "Daddy readin" the newspaper. We know that the newspapers *are* read by all our people, from the inhabitants of the Presidential mansion down to those of the thatched cottage with the ground for a floor; but we will look in at one of an average of the whole, on a winter evening, when the household are gathered around the bright, comfortable fire; every-thing within is neat, clean, plentiful and substantial, not the gorgeous trappings of the rich or the scanty appearance of the poor, for it is the average of the great whole. We see a large and happy family ranging from the tow headed boy that is paddling with a stick in the ashes, up to the grey-headed sire, who has been reading the deaths and marriages, a short paragraph or two on who'll be President in

'53, from the latest country newspaper. The attention of the circle
is at last brought to a listening point as the reader drawls forth—
"Latest news from California," "Arrival of the steamer ——,"
with —— passengers and nearly three millions of dollars in gold
dust. At the mention of the millions of dollars, two or three *big* boys
jump up and gather closer around "old dad," and ask to hear *that*
again. The universal California fever has been but lingering in the
systems of these youths for some time, but it now amounts to a
raging disease, and *go* they must. The old man, looking over the top
of his spectacles at the tallest *specimen* of himself amongst the boys,
seems to conclude that one "must go." The old lady thinks of what
things her first born would need on his travels; a sister or two look
at the destined brother, and think if they only could go along, what
"fortunes they could marry out there;" little tow head drops his stick
and asks his kind parent if he "may'nt doe too;" and, in short, California at this point is a great country amongst them. The reader continues with the news from California, down to "Life in California."
Under this head some *verdant*[1] out here has detailed to a *paper* in
the Atlantic States our horrid murders—the death of one *hombre*
by being cut in halves with an *infernal* great knife in the hands of
another man; two women and five men hung by *Judge Lynch* for
stealing; besides several other *desperate* things. This detail materially changes the opinion first formed amongst the listeners. The old
man drops the paper, wipes his "specks," heaves a sigh, and pronoun-
ces it "dreadful." "Marm" declares that John shall never go to any
such place, where he *mout* be killed or hung for "nothin' on airth;"
John's face becomes the length of that of a mule's, and his whole appearance seems to say, *I won't go;* the sisters (God bless them) lose
all ideas of taking husbands from amongst "such a set," and little
"tow head" has become frightened and sent off to bed.

It is not the writer's object to sort out any such details as the
above to fill a description of "Life in California;" but in detailing the
thing, as it is and was, some few such cases as murder and trial by
the *people's* courts will naturally occur.

---

1. An inexperienced person, a greenhorn.

As reminiscences of the past *life and times in California* proves interesting to our present community, we will go back to 1847, before *gold* had corrupted or altered California *natural*.

As the good old, quiet and picturesque city of Monterey was the centre of attraction in '47, being the *proper* seat of government, and head-quarters of the army and navy, we will go there for the commencement of some of our scenes.

Monterey, the capital of Spanish and Mexican California before the coming of the Americans. (Revere, *A Tour of Duty in California.*)

Monterey, being the centre around which some of the scenes of our California life is laid, a description of it and the adjacent country may not be uninteresting here.

It is situated at the head of Monterey bay, on a beautiful plain, which is scooped out of the pine-clad hills surrounding it. There is not in California a more picturesque or healthy place. It is one of the oldest settlements in California, being first settled in 1770. Nearly a century has passed since the first armed sons of Adam commenced the *presidio* or fortification under the banner of Cortez on the little knoll that overlooks the placid waters of its bay. Portions of the remaining walls of this fortification, and those of the old mission, which were built at the same time, are still standing. The present church, which now stands a monument of "times long past," is within the limits of the crumbling walls of San Carlos de Monterey. To stand amongst these mouldering ruins, causes thoughts of the past and

present to roll through our mind; we think of those who lived and
died within them, "long, long ago." Around the decay of a race nearly
past, arises the stately mountains which adorn the present city of our
destined race. Not only on account of antiquity, and the unparalleled
climate and loveliness of old Monterey, it is made dear to the heart of
every true Californian: it is the old capitol of *Alta California*. Here
the former race who governed held their counsels, and here the pioneers from the interior settlements flew for protection in the hour
of danger.

When our eagle soared aloft to view the goodly land for freedom's
sons, it was here she first found a resting place, and from her talons
let fly to the western winds our starry flag, beneath whose folds our
steel-clad warriors told a wondering world that Pacific's waves now
washed great America's western bounds. Not only was Monterey the
first place in California that the American flag was hoisted, but it
was the residence of *our* first governors, and from out its old walls
went forth the mandates to us to *govern ourselves;* from here a world
was told to come, that this was *Ophir;* and here, too, our model constitution was framed and signed. New things took from it the name
of Capitol, and removed it to San Jose—and since it was removed
from there, its ancient seat, it has continued to *move*—but, like the
prodigal son, as soon as its *wealth* has been spent in *foreign* lands,
in riotous living, and it has fed on *husks of corn* amongst swine,
it will return again to its present place in hunger and rags, and be
joyfully received by its father, who *grieved* for it as one that is *dead*.

Ranchos and Rancheros

THREE MILES SOUTH of Monterey is the Mission and valley of San Carmel.[1] This Mission, like all others in California, has ceased to exist, and its buildings, once teeming with life, are now a mass of ruins.

A feeling which cannot be expressed comes over the visitor to these old Missions; it is created by a mixture of sorrow and joy that is such as to make its experience a heart-felt pleasure. The old churches are generally the best buildings, and have defied the decaying hand of time better than the remainder. Their bells, which once sent forth melodious sounds to call their devotees to prayer, now hang silent. The owl has made its home where the sacrifice was once daily offered. Where are the old occupants who used to make these crumbling walls resound with busy, happy life? They have passed and gone, to make room for those to whom their lands have been given. The old Mission of Carmel is built near the sea shore, where the Carmel river enters it. The beautiful valley, the high peaks of the coast range that surround it, the pine forest that stretches far to the south, the wild sea that talks in thunder tones along its rock bound coast, all tend to make it a romantic retreat for the lover of poetic scenery.

The valley of Carmel is some fifteen miles in length, of inexhaustible soil, and in a very romantic dell, which is now thickly settled by hardy California squatters. A remnant of the Indians which once belonged to the Mission continue to reside on the Mission lands. As an evidence of the purity and health of Monterey and surrounding country, I may mention the fact that there are six of these Indians over one hundred years of age; two of them, whom age has withered

---

1. Misión San Carlos Borromeo del Carmelo—Carmel Mission.

until their frames alone proclaim them to be human beings, affirm that they were old people, and brought grandchildren to the Mission at the time it was built. They are both still able to go about, and are always found busy at some employment at their huts.

The Salina Plains, twelve miles from Monterey, is a beautiful body of land, twenty-five miles in its greatest width, and about eighty in length, of unequalled soil, and watered by the Salina [Salinas] river through its whole length. Large portions of this land is covered by Spanish grants, and the remainder is nearly all taken up by pre-emption claims. The mountains surrounding these plains abound with grizzly bear, deer, and hare, and quail, geese, many varieties of ducks, snipe and plover, are abundant in their season on the plains and waters in the vicinity. [In the Carmel river, at certain seasons, salmon and other fish are found in abundance and the mountain streams leading into the Bay and Valley, contain brook trout equal in flavor and size to those of the Alleghenies.]²

Under the blessings of all the beauties and fertility of soil which nature could grant around Monterey, it is not to be wondered that its inhabitants were happy; and a picture of life in 1847 in its vicinity, will give the reader an idea of "a ranchero's life" in California. The word *rancho* means here what we term farm in the East. But there is a great difference in size, ranches ranging from one to thirty miles square, according to the grants made to applicants from the Mexican government. These grants were chosen with the sole view of using them as grazing farms; they generally contain, however, some of the most choice portions of our agricultural lands. In most instances the owners of these ranches have erected large one story adobe houses, in which lumber of any kind forms but a small item of their composition, being covered with rudely made tile, and having the "ground for a floor." But few of these buildings have wooden doors or glass windows, a dried bullock's hide being used for the purpose of closing the apertures; such a thing as a chimney was never thought of in their construction.

The outbuildings consisted of rude huts, erected by the Indians, who were always found on the ranches, and who are, in fact, slaves

---

2. This sentence is from the 1852 book; it was not in the original newspaper article.

to the rancheros, but under the mild name of Peon. The principal
feature amongst these structures, is the *corral*, a pen on which much
labor is always expended. In their erection large and strong timbers,
some eight or ten feet in length, are used, the ends being sunk side
by side in the ground.

Near these establishments, surrounded by a rude fence, is generally a fine piece of bottom land, well watered, [called a *milpre*,] which
is used for the purpose of cultivating small quantities of corn, beans
(*frijoles*,) pumpkins, melons, and red pepper (*Chili colorado*,) —and
many raise considerable quantities of wheat and barley. The hills and
vallies in the vicinity were covered with herds of horses, cattle and
sheep—many of the rancheros owning from ten to fifteen thousand
head of cattle, from five hundred to two thousand head of horses, and
sheep innumerable. Their implements of husbandry consisted of the
California cart, comic old hoes, and a plow invented in the days of
Moses. This plow is made by simply taking the fork of a tree, cutting
one prong short for the stalk and leaving the other long for the beam;
the stalk is sharpened and plated with a small piece of iron; the beam
is left some twelve feet long, the end of which is made fast to the
yoke on the oxen; the lower portion of the timber being left sufficiently long, forms the handle by which the unwieldly machine is kept
erect. To work this "land divider," one yoke of oxen and two Indians
are necessary, one of the Indians driving and the other holding the
plow. Swarms of chickens and dogs, mixed amongst the whole, make
up the outside picture. The ranches, from their size, necessarily
placed the residences of the old settlers far apart, and each formed
a little community within itself.

The reader (particularly one of the *sovereigns* of the U.S.) who
has been used to all the comforts and conveniences which the arts
and sciences can render to man, will conclude from this picture that
pleasure and comfort were rather scarce commodities in the good
old times of "Life in California;" this, at least, was my impression
about those days. If happiness, in the full sense of the word, was
ever enjoyed by mankind, it was by the old settlers and inhabitants
here before the discovery of gold brought our present mixed *male
population* amongst us. Let us look at the life of one of the old
rancheros, as an illustration of the whole: he is a perfect model
of health, if anything generally tending too much to corpulency.

A man of high social position.

His dress is in keeping with the climate and the semi-civilized age of the country he lives in; his hat, composed of felt, made thick and strong, covered with black oiled silk, has a tremendous brim, with a sugar-loaf crown of enormous height; from its bullet-proof properties, it protects him from winter's rains and summer's suns, and likewise serves as a formidable shield in an encounter with the knife—in a modern phrase, it is a "hard old tile." His shirt, with its immense collar made of the finest material, has the collar and bosom fantastically worked with lace and ruffles. His jacket is fashioned *a la* man-of-war, and made of fine black or blue cloth. Pantaloons are of fine white cotton, made in turkish style, immense legs, the bottoms of which are confined as high as the knee by long white stockings being drawn over them; a pair of *calzones*,[3] made of fine material and faced with scalloped cotton velvet of a different color from the body, opened up the sides and adorned with silver buttons, is drawn over the pantaloons, and usually left open as high as the knee, and the whole fastened around the waist by a fancy colored scarf. The shoes are made light, of parti-colored buck or elk skin tanned by themselves. A gaudy colored *serape* that is always carried either by thrusting the head through the centre and letting it hang around the person, or carelessly throwing it over the shoulder or arm. His

---

3. Breeches or trousers.

A California party on a Pic-nic excursion. (Colton, *Three Years in California.*)

complexion, owing to the mixture of Castilian and Indian blood, is what one of our western boys would term "yaller," but on his olive-colored face sits forever the smiles of contentment and ease. Encase his legs in fancy-worked leather leggins, place on his heels a pair of immense spurs, and mount him on one of the finest horses, caparisoned with a silver mounted saddle and bridle, give him a paper cigar, a lasso in his hand, and you have before you a ranchero—"one of the olden time."

Having described the ranchero and his rancho, we must pay him a visit, to know how he lives. The visitor was welcomed to one of these old ranchos with an unfeigned cordiality that has now nearly passed away. You would be embraced by himself and wife, and told by him that his ranchos, horses, cattle, wife, children, servants and all he possessed were at your service as long as you wished to stay. The whole family also joined in this welcoming. The "whole family" in California means a great many persons, for it is no unusual occurrence to find twenty-five and thirty children the offspring of two parents, the mother looking nearly as young as her oldest daughter. The best the rancho afforded was provided for the visitor, especially if a stranger. The fattest of the flocks were always killed for food, the choicest pieces taken for the family, flesh cooked in different ways, *frijoles, tortillos* and tea constituted the general subsistence; milk and cheese were also in abundance. The meat of fat cows was always hung up in abundance, and a room filled with delicious jerked beef, so that the hungry about him might eat and be filled. The month of August, at which time animals of all kinds are fattest, was devoted on the ranchos to killing cattle for their hides and tallow. From five hundred to two thousand were yearly killed, their hides dried, the principal part of their tallow tryed out, the lean portions of the carcass cut in strips and dried, and the remainder boiled down and converted into soap. The hides, tallow, and soap formed the exports of the country, and was the only means for the ranchero to convert his stock into money. Yankee trading vessels were always on the coast to barter goods or pay cash for these articles of export. Bullock hides of good quality were worth $1.50 in cash, or $2 in goods. Good hides at that day, in fact, passed current for the purposes of internal commerce—they were California shinplasters, and they were the only circulating medium, not coined, ever used with us. The average price

A fandango in 1848.

paid for cattle thus sold, amounted to about six dollars per head.
With the proceeds of these yearly sales, the ranchero purchased fine
and gaudy clothing for himself and family, and a coarser supply for
the Indians in his employ, and also fancy horse equipage for himself
and children,[4] as the height of a Californian's ambition, consisted in
being superbly mounted. Thus surrounded by plenty, blessed with
health, money at command, no sheriff or taxgatherer to make professional calls on them, in the midst of their happy children, they passed
their time amongst their flocks, breathing the balmy air which is always laden with the fragrance from the flower clad fields. They may
be said to have sung and danced their time away. Picnic parties were
frequent, to which the young and old repaired, and made the dells in
the wild woods ring with merry peals of laughter; fandangos were
also of frequent occurrence, and the sound of the violin and guitar
scarcely ever died away at the old homesteads. After skimming over
the broad plains on their fine horses during the day, they joined in
the giddy waltz at night. It was of no unusual occurrence to see the
little black eyed girl of seven or eight summers, and her great grand-
mother going through the intricacies of a Spanish dance together.

---

4. The 1852 book replaced the word 'children' with *vaqueros*.

The Americans
and the Californians

THE FOREIGNERS IN CALIFORNIA, who had been in it for several years, were married to daughters of old rancheros, and generally rich and happy. The restraints of refined society and the bonds of civilization which they were used to in other lands, were here thrown off, and life and the pleasures of this world became doubly dear to them; their natural shrewdness gave them advantage over the native population that proved so beneficial as soon to place them in possession of equal wealth with their benefactors. Those who had been but a few years here, principally hunters and trappers, continued to live a free roaming life. Life in California, with them, might be termed the essence of human liberty. The climate being that of a perpetual spring, the hills and plains were as comfortable residences for them at all times, with the addition of a tent or lodge, as they could desire: they spent their time in hunting sea otter, (with which the coast abounds,) beaver, bear and deer. The skin of the sea otter was worth here $40.00 each, and were purchased for the China trade; bear and deer skins and bear's oil commanded good prices, and were purchased by the trading vessels on the coast. Monterey was the principal trading post for them, to which their furs were brought and sold. With the money thus obtained, they purchased such necessaries as they needed in the mountains, of which whisky formed no small item. After their purchases were made, they then indulged in a good old fashioned frolic, until the remainder of their money was gone— they cursed all things civilized, and left for the mountains again.

Of all the human family on earth, there are none to excel the hunter and trapper of the American continent in deeds of noble daring and personal bravery. Amongst hostile tribes of savages he has pierced the depths of the wilderness, thousands of miles in advance

A fur trapper, clad in his finest clothes.

of civilization—alone he has set his traps on the inlets that form the heads of the Mississippi, Missouri and Columbia rivers—fearless alike of the dangers from man or beast, he has pitched his lodge in the deepest recesses of the Rocky Mountains and the ice-bound shores of the northern lakes. And here, in California, even in advance of the Cross, he was to be found, hunting the fur-clad animals on the waves of the Pacific, or in Nevada's snow-capped hills.

To know how these pioneers enjoyed "Life in California," we must go to their homes in the forest. Far from any settlement, they pitched their lodges or built a rude hut on a pure mountain stream, surrounded by groves of timber. In the red wood forests, found in the heads of most of the valleys making in from the coast, those hunting otter, deer and bear generally took up their residences. Here, generally free from the trammels of law or restraints of refined associations, and knowing nothing of "man's inhumanity to man," they enjoyed the heart's pleasures that alone can be found in the picturesque solitudes of the mountain's depths. There is an ennobling lesson which is learned in the wilderness by the mountaineer of America, that places him, in principle, above the rest of mankind. From the dangers that surround him at all times, he has been taught to look on them, and even death itself, with cold indifference. Fear is a word they know no meaning to; and their rifles are ever ready to repel infringements or imposition on their liberties. They learn from the great book of nature, spread out before them the existence of one more great than they, of one Eternal Being who almost speaks to man while he is surrounded by the greatness of His works, on which the stillness of the wilderness has been unbroken through countless ages. If the human heart longs to hold communion with Heaven's King, it is not to be found in gorgeous temples, adorned with glittering tapestry, built amidst piles of palaces inhabited by licentious man; not where crowds of the sons and daughters of earth have adorned for gaudy show, whose hearts are filled with wrangling ambitions, even as they kneel on downy cushions before altars adorned in costly array; not amid the strains of earthly music and clouds of incense from burning censors can the heart of man be humbled to adore an Unseen Ruler! But go to the homes and haunts of the mountaineer in the lone forest, where the grandeur of Heaven's architecture surrounds you, where the music comes from babbling brooks, and songs of sportive birds, where the air you breathe is laden with the sweet perfumes from the flower-clad hills and vales around, which arise as a befitting incense for adoration; where the cloud-capped peaks of the mountains ever point into the azure vault above, and tell the heart there is a God. To this great being the mountaineer alone has veneration. They hold in derision anything like a government that attempts to check them in the full enjoyment of their actions; and they hold in contempt such things as officers of the law and the members of refined society; and the life of a mountaineer in California may be said to have been one of independent happiness, not to be met with elsewhere.

Having thus briefly noticed life in the settlements and mountains in the vicinity of Monterey, which serves as an exact representation of the whole of California at that date, we will take a look at city life, and all the inhabitants then here that have not as yet been mentioned.

The principal inhabitants who had deserted their homes in the towns on the coast at the time the Americans took possession in '46, for fear *Los Gringos*, (the Cannibals) as we were represented to be, would eat them up, when they found that plenty of their fat beef would appease our appetites, had returned to their homes, where they soon perceived that a cold roast *Greaser* did not constitute a part of an American soldier's or sailor's rations. The fear entertained of the Americans by the female portion of the natives, never could have amounted to much; at least the pretty black-eyed girls (God bless them) never ran from the approaches of the uniformed *hombres*, but on the contrary became almost fanatically attached to them. The officers of our army and navy who were in California, had no chance of displaying their prowess in the arts of war, or gaining for themselves laurel wreaths for deeds done on the battle field, although every occasion offered by the enemy for a display of their skill and bravery, it was such as their country expected of them, and more than Mexico wished for.

The native Californians soon became a part of *us*, and left the members of our army and navy in inglorious inactivity. The free and easy principles of both nations soon created a most agreeable and happy state of affairs amongst us. As all the towns were garrisoned, associations of the most intimate kind were formed between the Americans and Californians throughout the country, and together we eat beef and *frijoles*, drank *aguadente*,[1] sang and danced, and merrily passed the time away. The expenses of war had put money in circulation, and everybody had plenty, and want was a stranger. The never-failing supply of beef, which was to be had at all times for killing it, formed a store-house from which the hungry could ever draw; if clothing became scarce and not to be purchased, we went to the hills and savagely robbed the timid deer of its skin, which was soon made to encase the locomotive powers in an everlasting pair of breeches, or hid the contour of the upper man in the shape of a good old fashioned buck-skin coat. Fremont's army, in particular, were deeply indebted to the mountain clothing stores for their uniforms.

The inactivity this brought about, caused every one to devise plans to pass the time away. Fandangos were nightly given by the natives, in which all participated. Monterey was graced by the principal officers of the army and navy, who gave to the natives many splendid balls and entertainments, at which the elite of the country intermingled with the sons and daughters of "Del Norte." Many

---

1. *Aguardiente*—brandy.

Vaqueros rounding up cattle.

American ladies could also be seen at these festivities, gracing them
with their smiles; while crowds of the fair daughters of California
made bright the scene with lustrous eyes. In the giddy waltz, the
ranchero, in his gaudy native costume, was to be seen gracefully
turning the fair proportions of a western lady, while our brightly
uniformed officers supported the symmetrical forms of the dark eyed
daughters of *la belle* California. From the grey headed governor
down to the midshipman of a few summers of the American power;
the old ranchero whose pleasing appearance told the looker on that
many a fat cow had died on his account; Ex-army and civil officers of
the Mexican government in California, sons and daughters of wealth
and poverty there commingled together in happy unity—where whirling waltz made sorrow fly, to music's softest charms. Fandangoes
were also nightly given to a less grade where the b'hoys "did for
pleasure repair." The use of the bowie knife and pistol, although
worn as ornaments, were never used at a *baile* of the olden time,
in the manner in which more modern life has made fashionable—all
went to enjoy themselves—quiet and good will to each other was a
marked passion at every gathering, although those who composed
them consisted of different nations who were at war with each other.
Besides these, time was killed by hunting excursions to the adjacent
mountains and plains, where the abundance of game afforded the
sportsman ample chance to display his prowess, but the abundance
to be found, did not require any great skill to obtain all that might
be wished for. Many Bear hunts might be here described, where the
deeds, like all bear stories borders on the impossible; besides excursions for deer, geese and ducks, where the numbers slain would be
put down for a "hard 'un," but it is best here to leave a large blank
for the reader to fill up from his own figurative imagination.

The Newcomers,
and Life in the Cities

THE OLD PIONEERS talked over the beauties of the country, the fertility of its soil, and of the happy times in store for them, when, amidst plenty and peace, they could live in independence in this delightful country of their adoption—for they had come here to *stay;* but sometimes when they would stand on the shores of the Pacific and witness the rolling of the heavy breakers on the beach, they seemed to heave a sigh to think they had at last reached "no whar," and that there was no "out west" to go to when the settlers got *too thick.*

The members of the army had become attached to the country by the inducements offered them, and the pleasant associations they had formed with the natives, combined with independent, free and easy effect that this climate has on the chain-bound children of thickly settled portions of the east, that a determined resolution to stay could be plainly read in every face. It was a resolve with us that this was to be our future homes, if our dear old Uncle Samuel kept it; it was what we most desired; if not, then Gen. Castro's farewell address should be verified in regard to its being forever lost to Mexico.

Changes! changes! the world is always changing, and so must "Life in California." Time passed swiftly, happily away, until the gold discovery in the spring of '48 commenced a great change in the quiet state of affairs under which we had lived. A new epoch in the history of the nineteenth century commenced with this discovery, which made California what she is, which is for the better, but those who knew her as she *was,* oft sigh for the good old times now past.

The rush from the settlements for Sierra Nevada's unexplored depths, that has been already noticed, at once broke up all our old quiet, pleasant associations. A depopulation took place in the towns and settlements to such an extent as to leave them in almost a deserted condition. What induced some of the old settlers to leave their quiet comfortable homes to adopt the miner's life, is unknown, as they had all their hearts could wish. But gold—accursed gold—the poisoner of the human passions, which is hankered after by us from the cradle to the grave, beckoned them to the hills, where it was to be had for picking it up, and nature could not resist it.

The gold discovery, although it broke up the old quiet life of happiness which had characterized the country for many years, brought about a state of equality of the people that is to be found in California alone. In this wide world, wherever civilization has made its paths, the struggle for the possession of wealth stands out as its pioneer. The possessor of gold, let his disposition be what it may, let his passions be such as to laugh or weep at the ills and distresses that the cold unfeeling hand of poverty afflicts on his species, he stands as a god of earth, a high priest of the deity, at whose altar the human heart alone worships. He can bid a world rejoice or weep. With its possession he can bid his species go to the ice-chained poles, or breathe the simoom's poisonous winds amidst the parching desert. With it he bids the father sell his child, the subject his king. With it he whets the assassin's knife, and dooms to death the victim of his displeasure. Prison doors fly open at the wave of his hand, and the hungry jaws of an offended law fall powerless at the touch of his magic wand.

The gulph that is placed between wealth and poverty in Christian lands is as great as that seen between Damon and Lazarus, and is so well known to us that we have but to cast our thoughts east of the rocky mountains to bring it vividly before us. This time-despised difference between wealth and poverty, has not as yet flourished to any extent in California. We are one people; the nature and climate of the country we live in prevent it; a free and uncontrolled use of our dispositions gives a stimulant to life, which cannot be enjoyed where the pleasures of life are chained down by what this world are pleased to term refinement.

In a short time after gold digging became a remunerative calling, society was reduced to a level. He who had from his political position or halls of wealth, looked down upon the masses of his fellow creatures as inferior beings, because they were poor, found that his position gave him no power over their actions, and the love of gold soon placed them pick in hand amongst the sons of toil.

In this way the people of California became at once one people, of one mind and calling; wealth placed them on nearly an equality, such as the world terms it. The luxuries of life were but few, and all the comforts to be obtained were accessible to all alike. Those who had been bound up in the straight jackets of polished society of other lands, on their arrival here in the land of gold, seemed in a great measure to change, as a snake does his skin—that is, the corporeal man slipped out from its old shell, and left the body to enjoy life, unbound and unfettered, as God had intended it to be.

The climate and free independent roving life of the miner soon alters a youth here, to such a degree that his kind papa and mamma would scarcely know their pretty child. The gold discovery appeared to be retained for the people who were in California in '48. With its discovery came the news of peace with Mexico and the consolation of California being a portion of the home of the starry flag. We felt it as home, and with all the pleasures we before enjoyed, gold to the heart's content was given us, as if to cap every desire that man is heir to. Under such circumstances, could a Life in California be other than a happy one? Could man long for anything else? Yet they did. Old associations in other lands, where gold would make them masters, not equals, they longed for again, and the cry of "I'll go home" still acted as a magnet to draw the heart away. This disposition to leave California is to be pitied, not blamed, for where is the heart that does not at times long to return again to old familiar scenes, to revisit "home," that dear old place. What a volume of recollections hurry up before us on the simple mention of "home;" let it be the gilded halls in the city's crowded marts, or the log cabin that stands in the wild woods, they are alike endearing to the heart. Parents, brothers and sisters, wives and children and loved ones far away, are seen during the dreamy hours of the mind's recollections, beckoning us to return, and in words sweet as the voice of Angels, bids us "come home,"—come home and revisit, at least for a season, those who hold us dear—revisit once more the graves of departed sires, the old play grounds of youth, the hill and dell, or city haunts of boyhood's happy hours. But to return to our subject:

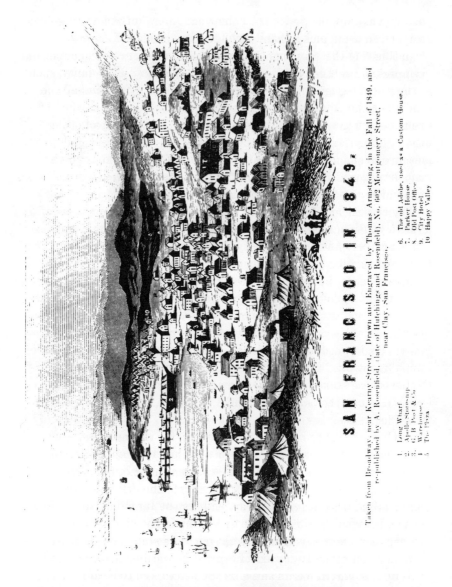

SAN FRANCISCO IN 1849.

Taken from Broadway, near Kearny Street. Drawn and Engraved by Thomas Armstrong, in the Fall of 1849, and re-published by A. Rosenfield, (late of Hutchings and Rosenfield), No., 602 Montgomery Street, near Clay, San Francisco.

1 Long Wharf
2, 3 Apollo Store-ship
4 G. B. Post & Co.
    Warehouse.
5 The Plaza

6. The old Adobe, used as a Custom House.
7. Parker House
8 Old Post Office
9. City Hotel
10 Happy Valley

Life in the cities during the winter [of] '48, was of a nature that beggars description. Yet there was enough of the old *leaven* left to prevent murder, robbery and theft being perpetrated—but every other vice that man is heir to, was fully indulged in—the immense quantities of money in circulation enabled the whole community to do "just as they pleased." The "nice young man" of other climes soon learned to drink and gamble with the most hardened adept of the "hard 'ns." Men who at home were regarded as strictly religious and temperate members of society could be seen *pungaling* down on old monte, while from the way *blue ruin*[1] had their eyes crossed, and their visionary powers magnified to such a degree, one card must have certainly appeared to them like a whole pack spread out before their choice. In San Francisco, where *life* was shown up in all its lights and shadows of deformity, merchants and speculators who were daily realizing thousands of dollars, owing to the entire absence of amusements, would for the excitement consequent, at times, sally out with a pocket full of "rocks," and amuse themselves by *bursting* up a few banks or with lively jests, let *slide* a few hundred ounces of the dust, just for the fun of the thing.

Gambling has been a ruling passion with too many of the inhabitants of California, since the recollection of the oldest inhabitant. I once heard an "old codger" assert that the first library brought here by the old Priests of the Missions, was a deck of monte cards. Cockfighting and betting on monte were the principal features of amusement or *sport* of the natives of the country. A monte bank was to be found from the Governor's residence, where hundreds of millions of dollars were staked, by men, women and children, down to the *five real fixens* on the *vaqueros* blanket, at which, a bullocks hide was considered a big bet.

The arrival of the first mail steamer in the spring of 1849, was welcomed by the thunder of cannon and the overjoyed huzzas of delighted thousands. It brought news from the Atlantic states only two months old, which was the *beginning* of the *future* short communication, when science and art will almost annihilate time and space. Previous to this, if an outsider was lucky enough to get a newspaper six or seven months old from the states, he stealthily took himself off and adopted a hermits life until he had read it "clar" through, advertisements and all. If he attempted to read it in a public place he had to take a stand and do it in a loud, slow and plain manner, or hold it up in a perpendicular position so as to allow an

---

1. An archaic term for gin, especially inferior gin.

immense crowd—front and rear—to aid him in its perusal. Before
the advent of steamers on this coast, communication with the East
was *via* Cape Horn or across the Plains. To receive answers from
the Atlantic states, to letters written here, in ten or twelve months,
was considered a fast line performance, although every exertion was
made by the military authorities to keep up a correspondence by the
shortest route and quickest conveyance possible.

A bullfight at Mission Dolores. (Gerstäcker, *Scènes de la Californienne.*)

Gambling

THE LOAD OF *adventurers* that came on the *first* steamer, to the
land of gold, were perhaps composed of a more motley class than any
that has since arrived. As they were the first emigrants who arrived
direct from home, or in other words, the first inhabitants that gold
coaxed into California.

A short description of the effect the climate had on them, and a
true outline of the *genus homo*, may not prove uninteresting. Having
been one of the "great unwashed," at Monterey, who aided in giving
them a welcome to California, when they first landed, an opportunity
was offered to become acquainted with the objects and callings that
many of them desired pursuing. They numbered nearly five hundred,
and were principally from the Southern states, although that inexhaustible storehouse of California emigrants, New York, was well
represented amongst them. All of them came to *dig*—provided they
could find nothing else that would pay as well and that would be a
much easier way to get a *pile*. Lawyers whose clients had been few,
had put off the dark garb and mounted a red flannel and the rough
rig of the miner. Doctors who had had but little practice and few
patients—and they all dead—had, botanically speaking, came to seek
the *root* of all evil. The unfortunate speculator had come to recruit
his lost fortunes by actual labor, if no other opportunity offered him
a chance to do it. Mechanics of every grade, and keen looking merchants intermingled in a mass that was moved by one impulse alone.
One fourth were professors of the "dark mystic sciences," in other
words, practical gamblers, of every grade.

As gaming is a prominent feature in California life, and no doubt
carried to a greater extent than in any other part of the world, a
short review of it will not prove amiss.

We who have come from the *second* families in Virginia, have been
taught to look on gamblers, and those who follow it as a profession,

as little superior to the devil himself. This view of the members of
the *black art*, may be good and just in other lands, but it is not applicable to California. To say gaming of any kind is not an evil of the
most to be dreaded description, would be to argue against common
sense, and all laws of morality. It is an evil—in California has become
a necessary one. It is, here, sanctioned by law, and its professors
constitute a large proportion of the first class of California society,
and one-fourth of the entire population of the state gamble to a less
or greater extent. Take the gamblers, that is those who follow it
as a profession here, and they constitute a body of men of noble
disposition, free, open hearted, and generous; and some of the best
improvements in the state have been made by the gamblers from
the proceeds of many a fool's money. The state also receives a large
revenue from the license imposed on gaming. To prevent gambling,
by making laws for its suppression in California, would be as useless
as it would be to stand in the Golden Gate and undertake to keep out
the tide with a pitch-fork. What a field for the study of human nature
is a gambling house! where the tenderest strings of a man's nature
are played upon, where the pre-eminent *and* prevailing dispositions,
and the hankerings of the heart for gold, becomes the master passion.

As the first steamer brought the first cargo of foreign masters in
the "mystic art," their annunciatory proceedings in California may
serve to illustrate scenes in a gambling house during the winter of
'48 and spring of 1849. Previous to this arrival, "monte" was the
universal game, in the cities and mines, interspersed at times with
"lump o' gold" poker. In the mines, especially in the Stanislaus
region, in 1848, I have seen the Spaniards, men and women, betting
freely pounds of gold dust on a card, and smoking cigaritos until
it won or lost, with as much indifference as if it had been so much
gravel. In the coast cities, (San Francisco in particular,) millions of
dollars were daily staked on monte, during that winter. The scenes
of these places of *amusements* have been shifted and a new set of
men have come on since then.

It required large capital to become a monte banker, as a small
concern would be *tapped* by almost any rough looking *hombre* you
would meet, during that golden reign. Large banks had their crowds
day and night, at which some rich scenes were to be witnessed. One-
half the betters were men who, a few months previous, would have

considered their characters ruined forever if they had been seen in
such places, were now to be seen "pungling her down," with their
heads presenting a mass of hair and beard that would vie with that of
Nebucadnazzar's on his return from his country sojourn spoken of by
Daniel, and around which fell in graceful folds portions of the brims
of hard worn "old tiles" from under which the only thing human to be
seen was the end of a "jolly red nose" and a pair of eyes sticking out
like a boiled crabb; Greasers wrapped in the *inhabited* folds of the
everlasting *serape*, only watching for a "sure thing," on which to pile
down a few pounds of the "oro." The rather trim appearance of a few
business men could also be seen mixed with the crowd of betters
provided the bank was a "good thing;" jolly sons of old Neptune, who
had adopted a country life in California for convenience sake, could
be heard cursing a losing card; and occasionally a bag of dust would
be passed in by a son of Afric, who acted as an outsider. A good house
would have four or five of these tables in full operation in it at once,
each with its crowd of devotees. A bar the whole length of the establishment, was the next prominent feature, where "old red-eye" was,
under his different names, issued in a perfect stream to thirsty suck-
ers at fifty cents per glass. Collected in the corners were small parties, who only loved to gamble so far as to play "old sledge" for
the liquors, until from their winnings they became so essentially
"corned" as to make a hard plank or the ground, when they retired
to rest, appear "soft as downy pillows are." Groups collected around
old *topers* to hear them sing songs. A pair of dirty lumps of mortality,
who had met after a long absence, commenced *wetting* the ties of
"Old Acquaintance," until they had become so loving as to hug and
kiss each other. A poor devil who had been on a *bender* too long,
might be seen out-shaking Belshazzar, and trying to hide from things
more dreadful than "Mene Tekel" which he thought he could see upon
the walls. A few overpowered by the *fatigues* of the place piled up in
a corner completed this faint picture of a California gambling house
in '48.

During the reign of this state of affairs, the *professors* before
mentioned made their appearance from the decks of "California."
The billiard rooms in Monterey were the stages on which they made
their *debut* into El Dorado. That quaint old place which had seen
many a little old fashioned monte bank give way before the power

Gambling at the monte table. (Borthwick, *Three Years in California*.)

of long bags of dust, was made to resound with a voice which told us
plainly that old things must change. These gents brought new games;
the billiard tables were stripped of their cloths, and converted into
tables for the different games, and stands for those who wanted to
auction off extra clothing, guns, pistols, and the most approved
Bowie knives. Monte, roulette, faro, ABC, twenty-one, and the sweat
cloth,[1] had their representatives, who (a new fashion at the time,)
praised their different *ounce catchers* up in something after this
style: "Here, gentlemen, is the monte bank that will stand you a 'rip;'
walk up, you chaps with the long bags o' dust; jest bet what you
please—it'll all be paid; pungle 'er down punglee!" "Here, you good-
hearted fellows, is the man 'vid de weel'—brought this 'ere fixens
all the way from home jest to give you something to amuse you; this,
genteels, is vat you calls roulette, the only game vat pays twenty-six
times for one; you can just bet where you please—on any number,
column, red or black side, or on the eagle bird; walk up, gentlemen,

---

1. Chuck-a-luck, a game played with three dice.

and make your bets—if you think I would cheat, why you can jest turn the wheel and roll the ball yourselves." Twenty-one would have its devotee using his powers to increase the size of his circle of betters. Faro would be extoled for its age and respectability, and the only fair game in the house, the dealer having no earthly advantage but the *splits*. The man having the sweat-cloth being a genius of the society whose members are known as "one of 'em," held a crowd around him; he was one of the comic characters we see at times, who come on the stage in this great drama of life and divert the lookers-on for a season, and then pass off. The inside of the house being full, he had to establish himself under the portico in front. The rainy season was not over, and the gentle showers which we see falling here at times, were descending in soaking torrents. In order to allow his betters a fair chance, he was standing outside directly under the droppings of the eaves that were running in perfect streams over his tarpaulin hat and India rubber coat. His cloth was spread on a bench in front of him under shelter, to which he called the attention of the outsiders by slapping his sides and imitating the crowing of a cock; and in imitation of scenes in other lands, he would, with comic gestures and a stentorian voice, cry "oysters! fresh clams! hot corn!" and many other kinds of commodities that California had never been

A faro table at the mines. (Borthwick, *Three Years in California.*)

blessed with. This idea took—soon a perfect crowd surrounded him, when he commenced to inform them that he had for his own amusement, and for the benefit of the community at large, opened the good little game of 'sweat,' a little republican game that all could play at— "jist walk up, ride up, tumble up, any way to get up; then stake up and win a fortune—I don't belong to the aristocracy—I don't; I'm jist a plain old devil like all of you—I am! and if you jest bet on old Ned's little game, you'll win—you will! and if any one gets broke, I'll give him money to get a big drink, sure!" At this offer an *hombre* stuck down a quarter of a dollar and lost;—"There, Uncle Ned," says he, "I'm busted—just give us the four bits for the liquor!" Ned, to make his promise good, forked over the half-dollar, (the price of a drink,) remarking, "you got me there a leetle—you did!" And thus continuing, he kept the crowd around him in a state of merriment that was new. To use one of Ned's phrases, "when them banks left, they were none of them broke—they wer'nt."

The reader must excuse this long description of gambling and gaming houses; but in giving sketches of California life, it could not be avoided, for it is one of the most prominent features in them.

Money, Crime,
the Law, Fast Living

THE UNHEARD OF QUANTITIES OF MONEY in possession of every
one, surprised the new comers to such a degree as to increase the
gold fever that had been consuming them, and every exertion was
made by them to get off to the mines.

At that time, getting to the mines was not so pleasant as it is at
present. Persons commencing from the South, during the season of
high water, made a pilgrimage via Benicia, and then up the western
side of the Sacramento to Sutter's Fort with pack mules and California carts. Those from San Francisco went by water, in every species
of floating vessels, from a ship to a "tule balza."

Most of these emigrants were men who had seen better days,—
gentlemen possessing that high-toned chivalric disposition that is
adherent to the South, and to be met with in southern life. Many left
by pack trains for the mines immediately on the steamers arrival at
Monterey, but the majority continued on to San Francisco, to take
their chance by water. Means of transportation were scarce and dear,
but if a man landed at San Francisco or any of the other ports in that
interesting situation commonly known as being "hard up," he had no
need to remain so, for he could get work, for which he was paid from
$15 to $20 per day, and be kindly thanked for condescending to labor
for that price, so that the means were always at hand to procure
enough of the 'needful' to pay his passage up the rivers on a launch.

As an instance of the commencement of "fast progression" in
California that the arrival of the first steamer foreshadowed, there
were two worthy mechanics amongst her passengers, who, after
having heard of the different modes of reaching the mines, determined to outstrip competition of every class, and for that purpose
built a small boat themselves in San Francisco, into which they

packed themselves and such necessaries as they required, and started for the southern mines. A month after bidding these enterprising men adieu at Monterey, I chanced to strike the Tuolumne river several miles above the plains, and at a point that I had no expectations of meeting a white man at that time. On reaching the river I found the two gentlemen above-mentioned, established in quite a snug manner on the bank, having navigated in their frail *bark* the Bay of San Francisco, Pablo and Suisun Bays, the San Joaquin river as far as the mouth of the Tuolumne, and thence up that river to the place mentioned, being a distance of nearly three hundred miles of difficult and laborious navigation. They had established a ferry, and were digging gold in a neighbouring ravine, and kept a quantity of the *ardent* to sell to thirsty travellers at a dollar per drink, and in short, they were fast gathering the crop they came for.

A San Francisco bar scene. (Gerstäcker, *Scènes de la Californienne*.)

Among the thousands of good citizens that arrived during '49 and '50, there came a swarm of burglars, thieves, and master rascals of every nation on earth, amongst whom Americans were well repre-

sented. Where such a mixed population as California has ever presented have been thrown together, with no law to govern them,
anarchy has shown its dreaded hand. But here with us it has been
different or at least in a mild form. From July '46 to April '50 there
was no existing law for our government, with the exception of the
presumed law of Mexico, which was entirely disregarded—and the
laws of California that came into existence, during the first two years
of its administration, failed to protect life and property, or it may be
said to have prevented rather than aided the objects for which it was
designed.

Under the existence of such a state of affairs, the well disposed
and honest portion of our community had to combine, and by a rigorous but *just* course, keep down the high hand of the robber and assassin. In thus keeping our community pure by hanging thieves, robbers
and rascals, who came here for the purpose of defrauding the honest
and unsuspecting, we have, no doubt, been looked upon by the old
Puritans of the East, and every land of steady habits, as little better
than heathen. Let those who object to the course we have had to pursue, consider for a moment what our situation has been, and they will
applaud, not condemn our laws and systems. We were without jails
or prisons of any kind wherein to confine criminals. Many men who
were but little above devils incarnate in their dispositions, were
thrown among us. To let them shoot down and rob whom they
pleased, to let them enter our dwellings and take from us our hard
earnings, or drive off our animals and leave the wayfarer a-foot in
the mountains, is, in all, something that the great majority of our
people never came to California to submit to. If in other places, for
petty and grand larceny and highway robbery, imprisonment for a
term of years would be the means resorted to to rid the community
of these pests—but we had no such places to send them to, we had to
either have them for associates)r hang them, and as the latter was
the most *agreeable*, we adopted it. And if this course had not have
been pursued, anarchy in its most hideous forms would have pre-
vailed, and bands of assassins and thieves would soon have put at
defiance every means for their suppression. As an instance of what
a relaxation of the vigorous course pursued before the civil code of
the state became in force, we may notice the state of society in '50
and '51. The people depending for protection from the law and its

officers settled down into apparent security. Many robberies were committed, immence sums of money were taken by the strong hand from the weak. Companies of thieves drove off whole bands of cattle, horses, and mules, and went in force to the quiet ranches, in the face of day, and plundered them. If any of these were caught by chance and taken before the tribunals of justice, it was nothing but a farce, and the villains instead of being punished, were to be seen in the street brow-beating and laughing at those whom they had robbed. Our order-loving citizens being by repeated wrongs and impositions, and seeing themselves unprotected, were goaded by them into desperation. This state of affairs was not to be tolerated in a country where depredation had had previously so small a chance. To put it down and give security to life and property, the world renowned Vigilance Committee of California was instituted. This institution is no doubt a new feature in a civilized and *christian* land, where law and its *supremacy* has cost the people so much as it has those of California. But it is a consolation to the order-loving citizens of California to know that the thinking, sensible portion of the balance of creation had taken the sensible view of this state of affairs, and have not condemned this purifying institution. To aid in purifying the community according *to* law, and not in its *defiance*, has been the aim of this institution. The members of the Vigilance Committee that had its rise first in San Francisco, where the depredations of the lawless were most felt, is composed of our best citizens, and has been extended throughout the State. The laws of the State inflicts the punishment of death for murder, arson, and grand larceny. Stealing over fifty dollars will constitute grand larceny, and it is left optional with the jury to inflict the penalty of death, or fine and imprisonment, on those found guilty of the offences.

The Vigilance Committee in hanging those who have been found guilty of grand larceny, have been actuated by the best principles in carrying out the intention of the law. To take the life of one of our fellow creatures for theft, may appear to the uninitiated into California affairs to be a cruel and unjust law. But the "peops" of *christian* lands must really exclude Miss California for having such *desperate* laws, for the fact is we can't do without it.

The progress that California has made during the last four years stands unprecedented in the history of mankind. "Gold" has been the

talisman that has attracted to her shores since the summer of '48, a
population more diversified than is to be met with in any other portion of the civilized world. Owing to the expense of reaching this
country from all parts of the U.S. and Europe, none but enterprising
men (until recently) have been able to reach it. Every nation known
to commerce have here their representatives. Their political and
religious opinions of every kind becomes with us reduced to a state
of life and association that is peculiar to California alone.

The stimulus that gold gives to business of every kind, has here
made every enterprise undertaken reach a perfection that makes
our progress appear almost an impossibility. "Get rich quick," is the
watchword, and every one has acted up to the matter—many have
succeeded, and others failed in the attempt—but, to fail once is but to
open a more sure way for future success. If we fail at merchandizing,
try mining, if that don't pay—take a *rancho*—and we know *that will*.

There is a *fast* mode of doing business in California, that had to
be adopted to keep up with the times. As an illustration of *short talk*
business habits to be met with in our cities, towns and elsewhere, is
a conversation held between a worthy captain of a trading vessel,
and a boatman on the Stockton slough some time ago. The trading
vessel and her captain were making their first voyage to the thriving
city of Stockton, just as they entered the slough, were met by a gentleman in a small boat with his dog and gun, going to the marshes to
pass a few hours, (snatched from business pursuits) in killing ducks,
when the following dialogue occurred:

> Captain.—Boat, ahoy!
> Gent.—Hillo!
> Captain.—How far to Stockton? How deep and wide is the
> *creek?* What's the price of flour? What dog is that? What'll
> you take for your gun?
> Gent.—Three miles; twelve feet by seventy yards; twenty-
> two dollars, and rising; the dog *ain't* mine; and the gun *ain't*
> for sale.

Business is often transacted to the amount of thousands of dollars
by merchants and traders, in just about the same short handed manner of conversation. We are a *fast* people. If an incendiary sets fire
to one of our *fast-built* cities, containing fifteen or twenty thousand

inhabitants, and burns it up in a *fast* manner, we go to work and re-build it, over the smoking ruins in twelve or fifteen days in a superior style; an undertaking that may appear to the balance of *slow* creation as a *fast* job *fastly* done by a d——d *fast* people. If a *fast* rain falls and raises the gold-sand rivers so *fast* as to wash away the dams and other improvements built on them, by our *fast* working miners, it is again rebuilt in a firmer and *faster* manner than before. Our farmers raise crops of grain and vegetables *faster* which they *sell fast* at *faster* rates than any portion of the *fast* world we live in. We now have *fast* steamboats, *fast* horses, *fast* express lines, and some of the *"fastest hombres"* that can be met with, and in fact it requires a *faster* pen than mine to detail the *fast* way in which fortunes are made here. We have seen for the last four years people coming into the country *fast*—and for a time they went out of it *fast*. But now there are so many that like the *fast* place, that they have determined to remain *fast* in it for life. If an *hombre* gets tired of his *fast* life, just let him steal something, and he can get a free passage out of this *fast* world on the California, *Lynch & Co's. Fast Line.*

Strong Drink,
and Judge Lynch

B UT WE WILL NOT QUIT THE SCENES of Life in California from the gold discovery until the present time, without giving it a passing notice.

If the word "elephant" was properly known as to the purposes it has been applied in regard to California, the shortest and most plain manner to convey an idea of a Life in California for the last three years, would be to say, it was the "elephant" and "elephant doings" in the land of the "elephant."[1]

The morals of the people were such as could be expected in a community that was to be here met with, in which every nation had its representatives, all struggling for the attainment of great and sudden wealth. The reports carried abroad of the cut-throat inhabitants in Eldorado, caused every adventurer to come armed for "fight." Many a pistol, sword, and gun, that had lain for ages unused, were brightened up and made sharp, so as to enable the new comer to *cut* out his road among the *heathens* of the gold mines. The old inhabitants of the mines, had to be armed for the sake of protection from the Indians; and the rifle was also a means of support to the traveller not an age ago, in places where cities now stand, in this fast country. Owing to the immense quantity of game to be found, the American, with his rifle, had no occasion to go hungry, and the arms of the miners of '48 were used in killing game, and occasionally a rancheria of troublesome Indians; but they did not regard each other as food

---

1. "Seeing the elephant" originally meant to go to California, see the sights, and dig for gold. One who had "seen the elephant" had seen all there was to see, and was, therefore, experienced and sophisticated. The phrase later acquired the meanings of "to celebrate" and "to be seduced"—both of which are quite appropriate.

for powder, to such an extent as to go armed for the purpose of letting daylight into a man's "inwards" on every slight provocation.
The flood of emigration that soon set in, changed the state of affairs
to such an extent that every person believed his precious carcass to
be in momentary danger of becoming a target for some adventurer's
fire arms; self-defence being the first law of nature we soon became
an armed community, which has continued to be an increasing propensity until the present time. Arming a man's person with a Colt's
revolver and a fine finished Bowie knife, is now considered a part of
our toilets; this part of the dress has become so fashionable that a
California gentleman is not considered properly *dressed* to see his
friends without these *ornaments*.

A man spake these words, and said: I am a miner, who wandered "from away down east,"
and came to sojourn in a strange land, and "see the elephant." And behold I saw him, and
bear witness, that from the key of his trunk to the end of his tail, his whole body has
passed before me; and I followed him until his huge feet stood still before a clapboard
shanty; then with his trunk extended, he pointed to a candle-card tacked upon a shingle,
as though he would say Read, and I read the MINERS' TEN COMMANDMENTS.
(James M. Hutchings, *The Miners' Ten Commandments*.)

In addition to these marks of *civilization*, nearly every body
drank *whiskey*. This may appear a sweeping assertion, but yet it is a
melancholy fact; "they did." Let a man's morals have been what they

may in other lands, on his arrival here he commences a new career, to what he had been used to. Thousands who have been covered up with the thin cloak of religious habits, soon let it fall from their shoulders, and the man *natural* shown out in bold relief. The influence that the society of the softer sex has over man's rude nature, was not here to be met with. We were a strange community, and, in a manner, lost to every finer feeling of our nature. Far removed from every species of restraint on our actions—struggling to make fortunes in the shortest possible time,—being blessed with one of the most delicious climates in the world,—treading the earth whose soil was mixed with gold— and money at the command of every one who wished to pile it up— caused a loose rein to be given to the actions of every one, to a greater or less extent. The war with Mexico had just closed, and thousands, fresh from the fields of battle, and a life in the camps of *Mars*, were to be found in our community, with the same reckless intrepid daring spirit that marked their trail through the blood-stained soil of conquered Mexico. Under all these circumstances, is it not one of the wonders of the nineteenth century, that California escaped the most dreaded form of anarchy? Or is it not one of the wonders of the age we live in, that a community thus composed could be governed or kept in check at all? Yet it *was*, and is now kept more pure by the method adopted perhaps than any portion of the balance of civilized communities. The rigorous measures adopted in California for the suppression of crime, has become proverbial throughout Christendom, although of the worst description, it is yet an unavoidable one.

During the existence of the military government, under officers of the navy, every exertion was made to conduct civil matters according to the Mexican laws governing California; and the appointment of Alcaldes and Judges of "First Instance" was made to fill all vacancies in the Territory where elections had failed to do so. The laws under which these courts were governed, were only *presumed* to exist for the government in cases where they were admitted. Few Americans, or even the native Californians, that had cases of any importance to litigate but left them to the decision of a jury, who were summoned by the Alcalde.

It is a melancholy fact, that in the civil affairs of California a love of *gain* has ever been the prominent feature in all constituted authorities of government. All who have come to this country since

the discovery of gold, have come with the sole intention of amassing
fortunes in the shortest time possible, and then leaving it. It is but
recently that a tide of emigration has commenced to come, to make
this State their permanent home. The recent developments of the
agricultural value, as well as the inexhaustible mineral resources,
and our unparalleled climate, has induced this blessing to the welfare
of the State.

A man who accepted office of any kind, done so for the sake of the
unlimited emoluments to be derived from it. If the deeds done by our
alcaldes were recorded in a form for the inspection of the curious in
such matters, it would form a volume of the most astounding jurisprudence ever presented for the government of civilized men.

In '49, amongst many good men who arrived here, were to be
found thieves and cut-throats of the worst description. They here
found a community without law, getting along quietly, and in which
a rich harvest appeared to offer them a chance to put in their foul
sickles and reap. They also found that money constituted a safe
bridge for them to escape over from the deep chasm in which their
iniquitous acts placed them. Murder, robbery, thefts, and deeds of the
darkest die, soon became frequent, when it was apparent that some
action must be taken to suppress the perpetrators, or leave the weak
to be murdered and robbed by the strong, with impunity. For the
suppression of crime, in the absence of a properly constituted police,
the honest and respectable portion of the community kept a watchful
eye on the actions of suspected persons, until they had a good cause
to arrest them. On the arrest of a murderer, burglar, or thief, the
alcalde of the district summoned a jury to try them. If found guilty,
the punishment was immediately awarded.

A description of a few civil suits has already been given, and a
notice of a trial or two for theft must suffice in this much to be regretted state of affairs in the administration of justice, which has
made California notorious in the annals of jurisprudence. The first
execution in California for theft, has been noticed in previous letters;
it occurred at the Old Dry Diggings, in '48. The miners for a long
time had been robbed of horses, mules and cattle, until the attention
of the community was attracted by these depredations, and the
people determined to ferret out the aggressors. Many miners from
the neighboring diggings had purchased animals which had been

stolen from the vicinity and rode back, when they were reclaimed
by their owners, or very uncivilly taken away by bringing a rifle to
bear on the rider, with a gentle request to "jump down from there."
Explanations of where they got the animals soon pointed out the
thief, who was a Canadian Frenchman. He was taken, tried and
whipped, and gently requested to leave the neighborhood. During
the time he was being whipped he made threats of the most violent
character against all God's people, and the vile Yankees in particular.
Abusing an American, especially when he is at *home*, is rather a
tender undertaking at times, and the manner [in which] this son of
another clime abused all things republican was enough to have made
old Jackson leave his grave, if they had been spoken near his resting
place—and which, of course, did not raise the victim to any very
prominent point in the estimation of his hearers, who at once determined to see that he left as soon as he was punished. A few days
after this occurrence, and before his back had got well, he was again
caught in the act of stealing five or six mules and horses, the property of some of his former persecutors. A party soon armed themselves
and started in pursuit, and caught him some twenty miles on his way
towards Sutter's fort, and brought him and five of the stolen animals,
found in his possession, back. On the arrival of the party in the diggings, a cry was raised to hang him! hang him! without judge or jury!
But things were not done on such fast principles at that day as at
present, and the depredator was granted a fair trial. There was no
alcalde within a hundred, nor prison within three hundred miles of
the place. To expedite matters, a judge was elected on the spot, who
summoned a jury of twelve men, who had not suffered any loss by
theft in the diggings, nor held any personal animosity against the
prisoner. These men, with uplifted hands, made oath to decide according to the evidence given before them in the case to be tried. The witnesses were likewise sworn, and the trial proceeded. The evidence
was decisive as to the guilt of the accused. The newly elected judge,
in his charge to the jury, simply told them, that he had no law to
refer them to; that there was no law in actual existence for the
government of the people in California, and that the jury should
first find the accused guilty and then award the punishment.

After mature deliberation the jury found the prisoner guilty of
stealing, at different times, horses, mules and cows, in the vicinity,

and sentenced him to be hung until dead. The prisoner, when this decision on his fate was announced, told the assembled crowd, "to hang, and be d——d, and to do it quick." He then made confession to many murders and robberies he had committed during his life, for which he deserved death long ago. An hour was granted the doomed to settle his earthly affairs, at the expiration of which time he was taken to a neighboring grove, the noose of a rope adjusted around his neck and passed over the limb of a tree; as many men as could get hold of the rope then jerked his body high in the air, where it was left hanging for two hours before taken down, a lifeless mass.

This occurrence gave the rather unpoetic name to Hangtown, now called Placerville, in Eldorado county.

I am sorry to say that I might here continue to describe trials and executions by the popular voice of the people until volumes could be filled, with descriptions that would make some bless the deeds, while other scenes in the execution would almost draw tears of pity from a stone.

In a community constituted as that of California, the newness of the country, and its unprepared state for civil government, this deplorable state of things *could not, or can it yet* be avoided.

A public execution is at all times a solemn thing, but there is something attending the trial and death of a fellow man, where the act becomes the duty of those powers not constituted or sanctioned by the laws of civilization, that at once fixes the attention, and causes the inquiry to be more searching, as to the guilt of the accused, before he suffers by the laws of usage, than any other ritual by which man is tried. Owing to the causes before stated, there has been over one hundred men hung in California during the last three years by a *popular power,* that here has been necessary, and is as yet unchecked. This does not speak well towards a quiet and orderly state of affairs, but, out of that number, not one has suffered unjustly, or been punished without unmistakable evidence of their guilt. This state of affairs must still exist until the country becomes more settled, and the community more stable in its nature. The facility that felons have for escape leaves the law and the officers without the power to arrest crime, without the *vigilant* assistance of all lovers of justice and right.

Trial by Twelve of the Finest

As regards civil matters, we have been, and still are a long
way from being on an equality with any of our sister states. The
greatest difficulty here is that law is too dear for a poor man to purchase any of it. To go into law in California, without a small fortune
to back the undertaking, is all "darn'd" nonsense. Let a man be doing
well, and have even plenty around him, and commence a suit in one of
our courts against a defaulting debtor, and he will become as poor as
the bow of a violin, before he gets out of it. Owing to this cause, many
a bill stands uncollected, and suits of different kinds are given to
the decision of boards of administration. In many cases disputed
accounts, involving thousands of dollars, are left to the decision of
one or two disinterested persons, to avoid the immense expense of
a law suit. Although the market is well supplied with lawyers, yet a
poor devil that becomes so unfortunate as to require an *advice* from
one, has to draw the law out of him by the music created by rubbing
together a brace of California mint-*scads*.[1]

We might here notice what effect the power of legal proceedings
had on a California jury previous to the institution of our present
courts. Being in San Jose in the winter of 1849, while the first Legislature was in session at that place, a suit was being tried before the
Judge of the First Instance.[2] The point at issue being the title of a lot
of land in the town of San Jose, for which both the plaintiff and the
defendant held *Alcaldes* deeds. The dust, being a little more plentiful
then, than it is at present, the litigants had each *armed* themselves
with a *limb* of the law. It was soon made known amongst the "great
unwashed" that two "rale lawyers war gwoine to plead," and a

---

1. Newly-minted coins.
2. San Jose was California's first state capital—from December 1849 to June 1851.

general rush took place for the court house. To give the general
reader an idea of the whole affair, it is necessary to describe the
Judge and Jury. The Judge, like a majority of the judges in California
at that day, was a firm, honest, and just man, with good common
"hoss sense," but possessing very faint ideas of law, or the many little technicalities attending thereon. The jury composed of twelve
honest men, presented rather a rough appearance, for so honorable a
body. Eight out of the twelve had their waist belt adorned with
California *jewelry*, in the shape of six shooters and bowie knives; the
other four being Spaniards, had the tops of their leggins beautified
with the protruding silver handles of the never absent boot knife.
From the unusually healthy appearance of some of their countenances, it was quite evident that they had been in attendance on one of
the *wakes* nightly held during that winter of magnificent drinks in
the third House of the Legislature. The two legal gentlemen, who
had attracted the attention of the "unwashed," were duly in attendance. One armed, simply with a volume of the Holy Scriptures,
while his opponent came with a perfect load of volumes on Law,
which was the most attractive feature in the whole proceedings, as
the astute gentleman piled up the volumes before him on the table,
until it appeared as if he had the whole Congressional Library to
draw from, and some of that *vile* auditory went even so far as to
"larf." One of the old ones, whose buck skin suit, and unshaved and
unshorn appearance proclaimed him to be one of the old trappers
before mentioned, became indignant at any such displays, and informed the crowd that, "that 'war' too bad for honest citizens to
stand, for boys, I 'ev been tellin' on you, what this 'ere country would
be comin' to afore long." A kind of "that ar' a fact," approbation was
given to this opinion; quiet was restored, and the trial proceeded.
Numerous witnesses were examined in the case, *pro* and *con*, to
whose evidence the jury listened to with attention. At times a discus-
sion would take place as to different points in the evidence, between
the legal gentlemen, which was highly amusing to the outsiders,
many of whom actually had never seen a case conducted by Attor-
neys before, and such exclamations as "don't yo hear that;" "don't it
take them 'ere fellows;" "by gosh he's a hoss;" "he d——d;" and so on,
as the gentlemen either gained their applause or disapprobation.

The examination of the witnesses being closed, the attorney for the plaintiff was about to commence his argument before the jury, when two or three of those honorable gentlemen had to beg leave to go out a moment—and nearly all of them had the same occasion to leave. I did not see any of them drink ardent spirits, but they all went into a place where it was mixed and sold at that time. The jury being again seated, the legal gentleman opened his case in quite an elegant style, which was listened to with "hang mouth" attention; he turned to the jury, and to soft soap that body in particular, commenced by saying: "Gentlemen of the jury, I can't say that you are, physically speaking, handsome men, (a laugh, in which the court joined,) but I do say that I feel assured, from your sun-burnt brows and toil-worn hands, that you constitute as honest and upright a body of men as ever sat on a jury."

Juror—"Wal, we a'nt nothin' else, and I feel confident that your client's cause is safe in your hands."

The legal gentleman had all that rough assemblage on his side up to this point; but as he had never seen the elephant, he commenced to overhaul the numerous volumes of law that lay piled up in front of him, and after opening them at numerous marked places, he turned to the jury, and commenced by saying: "Now, gentlemen, I will read to you all the law bearing on this case." But, alas! Othello's occupation was gone. At the mention of *law*, a buzz of disapprobation was heard in the crowd, and the jury was almost thrown into spasms. The legal gentleman took no notice of this, but, raising up one of his books, said: "Now, gentlemen of the jury, I will read to you from Blackstone, vol. 2, page ——"

Juror—"No, you need'nt, we don't submit to any of Blackstone's laws here."

Juror, 2d—"No, nor Mexican neither."

Juror 3d—(A big burly looking man,) stood up, shook himself, blowed, something similar to a hunch back whale, and then sat down again.

The legal gentleman appeared to be 'set back over a feet,' and commenced a stirring appeal to the court for protection. The court, not being posted up in such matters, squirmed and twisted about similar to an eel in a frying pan. The judge lit his pipe, wiped his spectacles, and gracefully informed the jury that they must submit to hear the reading of all the law necessary in the case. The laws in reference to the case, from different commentaries, were then read, to a perfect inattentive and disgusted jury.

The attorney employed by the defendant, then arose. He had seen the Texas *elephant*, and knew well the course he had to pursue. He told the jury that he had a better knowledge of the state of California, than to think for a moment that such a thing as laws of any kind existed, with the exception of the accursed laws of Mexico, which he knew no true American would submit to. After a short but patriotic speech and eloquent address, he submitted the case to the jury, amidst a thunder of applause. The jury soon returned a verdict for defendant. The defendant was a white man, the plaintiff a *greaser*, this fact might have had some slight influence, but I guess not. An appeal was immediately taken.

The plaintiff and defendant had then plenty of money, and in 1851 the case was still before the supreme court. I saw the defendant, with whom I am acquainted, a short time ago, and gentle reader, he was the poorest white man I ever saw.

IX. Thou shalt not tell any false tales about "good diggings in the mountains," to thy neighbor, that thou mayest benefit a friend who hath mules and provisions, and tools and blankets, he cannot sell,— lest in deceiving thy neighbor, when he returneth through the snow with naught save his rifle, he present thee with the contents thereof, and like a dog, thou shalt fall down and die.
(James M. Hutchings,
The Miners' Ten Commandments.)

Satan and the Legislature

As THE [FORMER] IS A SCENE, in Life in California, during the session of the first Legislature, and within hailing distance of the State House, we might as well pay that Honorable body a visit, and make a few notes of the Life in a California Legislature.

As these sketches are not intended to go into deep arguments as to *causes*, a brief notice of *effects* will be sufficient, on the head of California legislation. If I wished to reach up and pull the cork out of the great inverted jug of wrath, and allow the showers of indignation to pour over me, I would say, that to give *employment* and *piles* to old broken down politicians and a herd of loafers who were too lazy to work, that had got into California, in 1849, this part of our old Uncle's dominions, became a State as soon as it did. The enormous debt, that stands like a ghost of our *departed reasons*, making each knee to quake, and eyes to start from their sockets, whispers with a hiss, *"you done it too soon."* What has California gained by becoming a state as soon as it did? In what respect has her people been benefitted by it? Has it gained us honor? Has it protected her people? Think over it reader and you will be led to *sin*, like me, in your opinion as to the *causes* that brought around the admission, in such a hurry.

Having had the pleasure during a short, but ill-spent life, to visit the Halls of Congress, and the sessions of Legislatures in different states of the Union, and there set spell-bound by melodious peals of eloquence, from a band of orators and statesmen, who stood without equals on earth, I was tied to the conclusion that all things would be right with California, if she could only get under the power of an American Legislature. But in these fond hopes, I am sorry to say, to use a vulgar phrase, we have been *"a leetle sucked in."*

San Jose was a wicked place during the winter of 1849 and '50. It was not only wicked on account of the unrestrained use of wine,

women and gaming, but then there were so many little comical plans
at work all the time, to worm the cash out of the dear unsuspecting
people for the officers in power. On my arrival in the capital there appeared to be a thick whispering in the air, a fœtid smell perceptible,
and when the breeze would stir the polluted atmosphere, broken sentences were to be heard, such as—"Ten thousand dollars for————."
"Eight thousand for ———." "Seven thousand for ——— ———," and
"Five hundred to each ———." "Twenty-two dollars and four bits, at
least, per day—ha, ha, ha," and other chopped off sentences, apparently coming from a bacchanalian feast, would intrude themselves
upon the ear; such as "gentlemen of the (hic) third house, I rise to
(hic, hic,)—point of order," "pass on another bucket of the anchor
brand," "how much, sir, do you suppose it will cost us to get that
measure through!" "We won't go home till morning, till day-light
does appear." Such mysterious sounds must have a source, at least so
thought the writer, and as the State House was the most likely place
to learn public and secret things, thither I went. When I entered the
hall of the second house of our first honorable Legislature, who do
you think I saw there, in all his majestic pomposity? Why gentle
reader the devil! yes, belzebub himself. The secret was out, the mysterious whispers in the air were explained—I knew it was he from
his personal appearance—and the company he kept. He was seated
at the opposite end of the hall to that of Mr. Speaker; in the centre
of his dear children, the sweet babes of the third House. There was
nothing unusual in his appearance except his coat and nose; in the
description of which the reader may see his lordship as plain as I did.
His coat was of fustian, fashioned *a la* sack, with immense pockets at
either side, and many others in different parts of it, of smaller dimen-
sions. The large pockets appeared to be inexhaustible liquor stores,
as all the members of the three houses seemed to draw continually
from them. Protruding from the smaller receptacles, in this noble
garment, might be seen the heading of different bills his lordship
wanted to present, and in one was a sample of state scrip—an article
he had opportunely thought of, for the benefit of his humble servants. His nose was the greatest feature to be seen during the session of that, and all subsequent Legislatures of this glorious state.
It was made of gold, and had to be the length of the hall so as to
touch up each honorable member, or at least a majority of them.

To make this appendage appear acceptable and its owner bearable it had divers fine specimens stuck on different parts of it, and at intervals it was graced by sundry bags of dust, thrown carelessly across its desirable proportions. You can readily imagine that a smeller of this description would have a great influence on almost any body of gentlemen, even those of very strong minds. As hard a nose as this, must come out of a very hard face; and this old gentleman's as well as I can recollect, resembled a pile of black trap-rock.

This being a new feature in legislation to any I had read of, or seen, I was curious to know how it worked, and so sat and witnessed the proceedings for a time. It was evident that the honorable members had to make a raise to pay themselves and all the officials, as long bills for board and liquor were daily being presented. The Treasurer had "nara dime" to pay out, and the question first to be discussed was a financial one. Money lenders were plenty, and the good people of California could have borrowed half a million at ten per cent per month, payable in ten years. This offer was made to the honorable body in open session, but as soon as it was brought up for consideration, I saw the use the long nose was put to. To have accepted this offer would have greased the wheels of government in too plain a manner, and would have allowed the people to have kept the machine moving too glibly and would not have allowed the babes of his satanic majesty a chance to speculate in scrip, so the gentle shake of the golden snout quieted the clamor, and from the pockets of his lordship's old coat, came forth a more savory and convenient plan in the shape of a bundle of pretty papers that only bore thirty-six per cent interest, and could be redeemed at *any time*.

When the bill to issue scrip came up, one hard-fisted member had the audacity to rise, and ask Mr. Speaker if that "are warn't a little agin the constitution." The words were hardly out of him, before the long nose was tickling his cheek; the specimens rattled, and bags o' dust slid up and down before his delighted eyes to such a degree, that he settled back in his seat. The idea of the state making so much money in one day, so tickled the honorable members, that the bill to issue state *shin plasters*[1] went through both houses, snapping and

---

1. Money of little value, based on inadequate security.

crackling like a burning hemlock plank. These papers passed for a
few days at *par*, then fell a *"leetle—"* just twenty-five per cent;—only
to try the thing. Members and feeders out of the crib, began to wear
long faces at the state of things; but *Nosey* soon showed them by
figures that to raise their pay a few dimes, it would make the sum of
difference come out just even. And it was a wonder to see with what
grace his Satanic Majesty handed out the fee and salary bills from his
great coat pocket, in which the members were allowed the modest
sum of *twenty-two and a half dollars per diem!* Those bills passed,
which was another great blessing to the dear people, which the shin-
plaster system brought about. Having seen the legislative elephant
sufficiently, and was about leaving, I saw Mr. Devil hunting up the
"Foreign Miners Tax" bill, and I hurried off to say a few Ave Marias
for my own salvation.

San Jose, the first state capitol building, 1849–51.

When the elders of the people gathered together again in 1850,
behold! Satan went also and took his seat amongst them. His great
golden nose had its old influence, and the specimens and bags o' dust
did marvellously work upon it. When he saw the effects his proboscis

had in certain water lot and usury bills, he became proud of heart, and desired to try his old offer of broad lands to make them fall down and worship him. We read in the good book of his Satanic Majesty offering our Saviour all the kingdoms of the earth if he would fall down and worship him; but his honor failed in the speculation. Not so with his California undertaking;—he told the great wise heads that San Jose was too mean a place for such devout servants to stay in, and he took many of them up into a high mountain—even into a high peak of the coast range, and showed unto them all his dominions round about. Some looked with longing eyes to the land of the mountain king—even to Monterey. But he said unto them, "Go not there, my children, for honey and wine are scarce in that land, and the frail daughters of Eve dwell not there." Being sorely tempted, they looked on the great valley where they had dwelt, even the valley of Santa Clara, and appeared loth to leave it. In those days, there dwelt in the land of Sonoma, a goodly man, whose name was Vallejo—a man devout and just, and one who feared God and served the Israelites— and the Devil tempted him. Being sorely pressed by the evil one, he was tempted to scatter many pieces of gold, even half a million of *pesos* amongst the wild oats that grew upon the mountains, where the elders of the land could go and gather them. And the Devil showed them this goodly place, near unto the great waters, in the land of Vallejo, where the gold was sowed, and where the elders who followed saw it; they all fell down and worshipped him, saying, "O, good and just Devil! thou hast ever been near unto us in the hour of our need, thy glorious snout hath ever directed our paths aright; and now thou hast shown us a goodly land, and we will go and dwell therein." And behold! when the summer came, to say the month of June, they moved the high priest of the people, and his household with the tables of stone whereon the laws were written, and the great ark wherein the treasures of the people were wont to be kept, from the palaces in the great valley of Santa Clara, unto the bleak hills that the elders had chosen, and did there pitch tents wherein they might dwell, for the *Temple* for their reception was not yet built.

When the elders were again to assemble in '51, the Devil was sorely pressed for a place for their gathering; but he gathered them together in our great city, to which the merchants of the earth are wont to bring their merchandise, even the city of San Francisco, and there chartered one of the fiery vessels that go into the seas, the ark Empire, to ferry them across to the land chosen for them.[2] This land was not pleasant to look upon, and the elders pressed the Devil hard to remove them, who listened to their grievings, and determined to take them unto a kindly place, where all their heads should become *dead ones*. And the place of his choice was the great city of Sacramento. The ark Empire having been an ark of safety to the elders during the stay in that land, was again seen ploughing up the great waters with the high priest and all the elders within her, which did sorely grieve the good man, even he who had sown the gold upon the hill, and even a widow's tears were shed on their departure.

In that goodly city to which they went, the rains fell and the floods arose, but they heeded it not, for the devil was with them, with his nose as bright and long as ever it was, and there he could be seen hauling from his pockets, bills for the sale of all the lands, that a kind high priest had given unto the little children for an inheritance forever. Cooley bills, and bills for a Tax on labor, are also held within his bird-like sinewy hands. And so bold has he become, that he has even dared to meddle with the free press of our people, and comes to take his seat with his pockets filled with printers type, that he offers to set up for the benefit of all whom it may concern. Oh! that our Elders would learn to fear the devil.

I hope the *Elders* will take no offence at this picture of "Legislative Life," in California, for they are aware that this devil does sorely torment them, at times. By the way, as we are speaking of Legislation, I would like to be present and hear an *hombre* introduce the Maine Liquor Law, for the consideration of our law-givers. God help any one that would undertake such an *Elephantine* project.

---

2. The city of Vallejo, where the legislature remained but one week due to inadequate facilities.

Getting Religion,
Progress, Social Reform

Religion of every kind has as yet formed but a small portion of California Life. Until recently, the Missionaries sent to this heathen land by different denominations have seen so small an opening for them, that no attempts were made towards the conversion of sinners. The climate had the same effect on many of these good men as it had on others less godless. They became good miners, soon learned to partake of the ardent freely, and became in a short time carnal creatures. Many of them not liking hard work, opened shops or dealt monte. Many may now recollect one of those who had once been one of the chosen few, who are *called* to spread the truths of the bible, who had a good monte bank in the town of Stockton some three years ago, at which he presided, and would quote scripture passages applicable to his employment. He was well fitted for the game being always cool and calm, and he said that he felt confident in the success of his game, as he had faith "greater than Peter's," in it.

Life in California at the present day, marks well the change that a permanent community has over a floating one. The change in affairs with us, has been so great, within the last twelve months, that those who were acquainted with California as she *was*, would scarcely know her as she *is*. Where we used to build a canvas city in a day, we have lately taken a whole week, and put them up of wood, stone, and brick. The miner who a few months ago had to pack his kit along almost imperceptible paths, can now find in their place, wide, well-beaten roads on which he can be hurried along in splendid coaches, at a rate such as is here required to keep up with the times. Where a short time ago it took from two to ten days to make a voyage in a launch up the rivers, to Sacramento and Stockton, it is now done in as many hours by fine comfortable steamers, and the fare and freight charges are also a shade less by these conveyances. From $30 to $50, had formerly to be paid for a passage, with the pleasure of fighting mosquitoes for a week, in an open boat, and the moderate sum of $400 per ton for freight. Steamers are now carrying passengers for $5, and freight at $4 per ton. The smoke of swift steamers rises like majestic monuments of commerce as they ply to and from the Bay, and inland towns, bearing full loads of freight and clouds of passengers. There is nothing more emblematic of the progressive spirit of the age than the rapid succession of improvements in steamboat building in California. The boat of to-day is superceded by a better one of to-morrow, thus boats that were "the pride of the slough," six months ago, now look as old and primitive as Noah's Ark. Should you doubt this, just step aboard one of those floating palaces, the American Eagle, Sophie, Kate Kearney or H. T. Clay, that "bile" but never "bust," take a view of their ponderous dimensions and comfortable accommodations, their cabins furnished in the highest taste of luxury. Then cast a retrospective glance on the little steamer Sitka, (the first steamer that ever ploughed the waters of California,) the San Joaquin and the Capt. Sutter, and you will think as I, old things have become new. The runners for these different boats will also inform the travelling public that their respective boats will beat any thing else up and down the river, or "bust." Such a recommendation would rather intimidate a less *fast* people; but here, any thing that will "beat or bust," is just the thing to suit. Any thing that is *fast*, and danger or adventure in the undertaking, will be grabbed at, with a "to h—l with the consequences!"

Things are becoming settled, and that wild ungoverned spirit of speculation, once so rife, has given way to a slow but sure policy, making a healthy business perceptible in our community. Under the old policy, the *old stock* of California amassed fortunes in a few *months*, which was lost in a few *moments*—not, perhaps, by mismanagement, but being too honest and unsuspicious, they were unprepared for the crowd of *smart* men who migrated to our shores in '49. These long-tailed gentry, who had lived on their wits in the land of "dog eat dog" policy, saw, on their arrival in California, that one of the softest things ever offered to their peculiar propensities, lay open before them. With their hard faces, which had been "run" so long that they had become perfectly smooth, and tongues calculated to beguile even the devil himself, they had but little difficulty in getting any quantity of goods on a short credit from our old merchants; those they took into the mines, and sold to the best advantage, proclaimed themselves "bursted," and immediately left for the east. They found it no difficult matter to "ring" themselves into the unsuspecting affections of honest yet wealthy men—men sufficiently honest to believe everybody else so. Thus some procured loans and advantages that made their stay in California a short one, for as soon as they had managed to swindle the unsuspecting out of all they required, they declared themselves bankrupt, and left. Through such means the first fortunes made in California passed into hands that never labored for them, and the just possessor left *broke* "flat, flater, flatest!" The quick way in which this was done, for a time threw our

X. Thou shalt not commit unsuitable matrimony, nor covet "single blessedness;" nor forget absent maidens; nor neglect thy "first love;" —but thou shalt consider how faithfully and patiently she awaiteth thy return; yea, and covereth each epistle that thou sendest with kisses of kindly welcome—until she hath thyself. Neither shalt thou covet thy neighbor's wife, nor trifle with the affections of his daughter; yet, if thy heart be free, and thou dost love and covet each other, thou shalt "pop the question" like a man, lest another, more manly than thou art, should step in before thee, and thou love her in vain, and in the anguish of thy heart's disappointment, thou shalt quote the language of the great, and say, "sich is life;" and thy future lot be that of a poor, lonely, despised and comfortless bachelor.

A new Commandment give I unto thee—if thou hast a wife and little ones, that thou lovest dearer than thy life,—that thou keep them continually before thee, to cheer and urge thee onward until thou canst say, "I have enough— God bless them—I will return." Then as thou journiest towards thy much loved home, with open arms shall they come forth to welcome thee, and falling upon thy neck weep tears of unutterable joy that thou art come; then in the fullness of thy heart's gratitude, thou shalt kneel together before thy Heavenly Father, to thank Him for thy safe return. AMEN—So mote it be. (James M. Hutchings, *The Miners' Ten Commandments*.)

commercial affairs into a ruinous mass; but it afforded the business portion of our community a chance to learn a lesson that in the aggregate has been of great benefit to business at large, and caused that sure and settled policy to be adopted which now marks the business pursuits of our people.

A social reform is also perceptible. This is no doubt owing to the increase of a female community, the absence of whose soothing influence on man's coarser nature, had here almost caused us to forget the gentler traits of our existence. A short time ago, if an *hombre* was lucky enough to get sight of a white lady, he talked of it for a fortnight afterwards; her personal appearance was noted, the dress and bonnet she wore minutely described, and wind up with a heartfelt wish to possess her "for better or for worse." It was a great country for old maids and *vidders* in those days, as age or beauty had but little to do with a matrimonial question—if she were a *woman*, that was all that was requisite. But at the present time our eyes are gladdened with the sight of great numbers of "God's best gift to man" daily arriving amongst us, and a man *vat* wants to marry, can get a handsome "white gal" for a wife. As we are speaking of the ladies, the "California widows" to be found in the east and all over the world, ought not to be forgotten. There is no doubt but all the men in California who have families in distant lands, are not neglecting them, but making fortunes for the purpose of giving them ease and comfort in after life, or striving to obtain the means of bringing them to this country. Cases of neglect and abandonment may be found, but it is of rare occurrence. This is not the case with *all* the "vidders" of our diggers, many of whom forget their dear husbands in California, for "may be" they won't come back again! We see several cases of this mentioned in the eastern papers, and the perusal of a letter written to one of our diggers, may go far to show a neglect at home as well as abroad. Many a good, honest man here can not read or write, and the one to whom this letter was addressed was one of that class. He was therefore obliged to get a confidential friend to read his letter for him. It appears he had been married in the spring of '49, and the honey moon had scarcely passed before the gold fever carried him off—not to the "cold hole," but to California. Arrived here, he had regularly made remittances to his absent dear one, to the amount of several hundred dollars. The letter here mentioned was written to him two years after he left his fair one, and was something after this fashion:

Dear Husbin—O my dere——I hav a mity site o' nuse for yu, the fust is yu hav such a fine sun—I had him next sunday com a fortnit, an o dere——he is jist like you for all the world—the very picter of his dere dada the tu hundred dollars yu sent me last I got from Mr. —— which makes me so hapy—my dere I du lov yu so much I cant slepe O nites an yu ort too cum hom to se me and morso now yu hav sich a fine sun Mrs. —— the old hag insulted me tu when I wer sic an sade yure prity baby wernt yorn case yu had bin gon to long away but she is only jelis case you ar beter off than hur husbin. do dere —— rite tu me an tel me when yu ar comin case I alwais thinkin on yu mister —— sends his luv too yu he has alwais bin cind tu me If yu hav eny more munny too send me you can cend it tu mister —— for me as i want it no more at pressent but i remane yure tru an loving wife.

Poor thing! No doubt but if *evil* eyes could be allowed to pry into every body's letters, that many such loving little epistles might be read. Many men who have been here and made fortunes and left, are now fast returning with their families, or with wives at least, to make this their permanent home. Comfortable homesteads are now

VII. Thou shalt not grow discouraged, nor think of going home before thou hast made thy "pile," because thou hast not "struck a lead," nor found a "rich crevice," nor sunk a hole upon a "pocket," lest in going home thou shalt leave four dollars a day, and go to work, ashamed, at fifty cents, and serve thee right; for thou knowest by staying here, thou mightst strike a lead and fifty dollars a day, and keep thy manly self-respect, and then go home with enough to make thyself and others happy. (James M. Hutchings, *The Miners' Ten Commandments*.)

to be met with at every turn. If a man comes to California and stays
two years, he will never want to leave it. As an illustration of what
makes the old stock return to California, I will relate a conversation
verbatim between the writer and one of the diggers of '49, who had
just returned with a fair bride, and which will also illustrate California etiquette. The last time we saw each other was on the head of the
Calaveras river. He had been in California seven months, and had
made over eight thousand dollars. The diggings he had, had become
worked out, and being unsuccessful in finding others as rich immediately, he was sitting in his camp cursing California and everything
in it, and pronounced it one of the *infernalist* holes a man ever got
into. From his manner then, I regretted to think that California was
about to lose one who would make a good citizen. He held on until
some time in '50, and started "hum to York State," where, the sequel
shows, he could stand it but six weeks; and in that time made love to,
and married a fair one to share his joys and sorrows through life. He
was the last man I ever thought to have seen returning. When we
met, the following salutations and explanations took place.

Writer—"Hallo! is this you?"

Returned—"Wal, it an't nobody else—how are you, old stock!"

W.—"So, so. In the love of God, what brought you back? when did
you come? I never expected to see you here again."

R.—"O, Lord! I've been back more than a year. Couldn't stand it
there, I'll swear."

W.—"Why? what was the matter?

R.—"Wal, old cock, the fact is, the people there are so cussed
mean, that a man who has ever lived in California can't stand it
amongst them. I hadn't hardly landed from the steamer in N. Y.,
before a perfect swarm were around me, trying every means to
swindle me out of all, or part of my dust; some of them got so very
near and kind around me, that I had to draw old *sixey*, and tell them
just look down the barrel and see if they could see anything *green* in
her bottom! And don't you think, *even* for that, I had to 'cut out' or
get put in jail. Oh, C—st! such a place you can't think on."

W.—"Well, it an't so bad in the country, is it?"

R.—"Wus, a damn sight! Even my own relations tried their pret-
tyest to get all the dimes away from me. I didn't see anybody that I

was ever acquainted with, who did not want to sell me something, from a farm down to a d—d old second handed coat!"

W.—"So, you left? what are you at now?

R.—Yes; I got my gal and left them diggins as soon as God would let me. I've got a ranch up the river now; got plenty of horses and cattle, pigs and chickens, raise just what grain and vegetables I please, got plenty of money, and in fact, I'm as happy as a clam at high tide!"

This is no single instance of this kind—so far from it, that it is a daily occurrence; every steamer brings hundreds of the same sort.

We find our cities graced by many edifices for public worship, which are becoming well attended. Each denomination is represented; but as to the number of communicants, it is not best to say any thing at present. It will no doubt be better after a while. Religiously, politically and financially, California may be said to be deistical, democratic, and *damned!*

Ministers of religion must live, as well as other people, and in California they doubtless have no fixed salaries allowed them by the members of their different persuasions, to keep them above want; to remedy this deficiency at the close of each religious service they pass around "that plate" for contributions, and on it the "good of heart" pass many a lump. But it appears somewhat singular that when the mines were good, and much gold to be had for a little work, the priests of every persuasion allowed the devil to walk up and down among the people, just as he pleased, without their trying once to head him off; yet now, when his Satanic majesty has in a measure set himself down to rest, and gold is *all-fired* hard to get, we find such a number of good men trying to roust the old gentleman from amongst the *heathen* now gathered here. But this is no doubt on account of the climate, and the great change that has taken place.

We sometimes see churches let for other purposes than for divine worship. For instance, in our inland towns if a board of Ethiopian Serenaders are short of a place in which to give *darkey* exhibitions on scientific principles, they have often been "kindly tendered" the use of a church. On the other hand, if a minister of the gospel takes a trip through the mines, and desires to point out the only *sure* way for the miners to obtain everlasting life, one of the best and most capacious gambling and drinking saloons is "kindly tendered" *him* for *his* performance. In these the paraphernalia of the devil is kept in full operation until the minister wishes to commence his services, when the landlord informs the crowd that the "Rev. Mr. —— is going to *preach* here tonight," and requests a cessation of present operations until after service. At this request every evil thing ceases in a moment—the gambling tables are set aside, and the devotees of the bar go dry until after service. Passing round the plate in these places, after preaching is over, pays well. As soon as the congregation is dismissed, the gaming tables are spread again, the bar opens, and things go on as swimmingly as ever. This is also on account of the *climate!*

A miner's life in California is what it ever has been—one of profit, independence and pleasing excitement. His home is ever amid the majestic scenes of Nature, surrounded by all that is noble and grand; his ears are ever filled with the limpid cadence of crystal streams that rush through mountain gorges, over gravelly beds rich with glittering treasure; the deep silence of the mighty hills that guard his home, soothes him to rest when the toils of the day are o'er, and no task-master's voice is heard at early morn to bid him go toil for a pittance from the hour when Aurora breaks the darkness of the eastern sky until darkness discharges him from his task. His time is his own; there is no one to bid him come or go; his labors are ever remunerated like those of a prince; there is an excitement ever attendant upon his exertions that makes work a pleasure, and he knows that the gold which glistens in the earth he is shaking up from its sleep of ages, will give him all the longing heart can desire in the shape of earthly comforts and pleasures. If he gets but little for a time, there is no discouragement perceptible upon his toil-worn brow, but he hourly hopes to find more; he ever thinks of striking at some hour a vast heap, that will place him in independence forever. He sees many hundreds who have been thus blessed, and this hope of success has a firm foundation, which disappointment fails to destroy.

At the present time the miners have within their reach every comfort that money can procure. There is an abundance of every description of provisions and luxuries to be had in the mines of California, at prices ranging only a shade above those of the coast cities; clothing can be had in California as cheap as at any other place in the world. The miner, although compelled to do more work for less gold than formerly, has the aid of every invention of art to assist him.

A great moral reform is perceptible throughout the State, with the exception of crime and its hasty punishment. In the olden time, every place where liquor was for sale was continually thronged by thirsty customers, and to meet one of the "unwashed" when not engaged in business, without his being considerably *corned*, was to see him entirely at variance with the fashions of the day. The gaming tables were ever crammed with betters, staking hundreds on the turn of a card, and winning or losing with perfect indifference. If they lost, they would tell Mr. Monteman that they would be back shortly and give him another *rip*, as there was plenty more up in the ravines. But a great change has come over this scene, also. Gaming tables we have, plenty of them, but they amount to a perfect burlesque upon what they have been. Although every exertion is made to attract crowds to the drinking and gaming houses, it fails to pay as it did a short time ago. These houses, instead of being the filthy holes they once were, are now gorgeous saloons, fitted up in magnificent style, with every costly and gaudy decoration the fancy can picture; bands of music "discourse sweet sounds" to attract the passer-by; young and beautiful women sit as bankers at the gaming tables, and as attendants at the bar, to deal out blue ruin with their fair hands to those who are athirst—but it all fails to arouse the old spirit once so vivid, which characterized a California community.

These saloons are crowded with a motley crew each night, but they do not congregate there for the purpose of drinking or risking their money in games of any kind. It is amusing to one who has seen the elephant from his infancy up to his full growth, to look on for a time at one of these saloons. What a picture of frail humanity is there spread out for contemplation! Every nation on earth has there a representative. In former times, betting heavily at any of the games failed to create much excitement among the crowd with which such places were filled; but at present, gambling has died away to such an extent that if an hombre goes to one of the tables and commences to bet fifteen or twenty dollars at a time, a general rush of the outsiders takes place to the table, to witness the feat. In a few moments humanity is piled around the table to the depth of ten or twelve feet. Oh! that we had a Hogarth, to paint in life-like colors one of these crowds. How such a painting would be sought after in other lands by those who have never been upon the trail of the elephant. There can be seen the clean-shaved, well-dressed man of business; the old Spaniard, with the pleasures of the game lighting up his countenance with the fires of excitement; sons of the *Republic la belle France*, with keen eyes peering out of a mass of hair and beard; the un-shaven, grizzly-bearded, slouched-hatted old Mexican desperado; the smooth-faced Indian, with gaudy-colored ribbons adorning his glazed hat; the black visage of a long-haired Lascar; the elliptical eyes of several sons of China, with their grotesque dresses and shaven heads, whose crowns are adorned with the ever-present *tail;* the broad-faced son of the *Faderland;* the ruddy face of the son of the Emerald Isle; the bushy head of the Kanaka; the bearded faces of Jew and Turk; the Chilian with his never-absent *poncho;* the tall, raw-boned frames of our Western men; Russians, Austrians, Hun-garians, Hottentots, Egyptians, Mormons, Mahommedans, Greeks, and all the varied worshippers of wood and stone, are here repre-sented—and, all combined, forming one of the pictures of life in California that must be seen to be appreciated. Not there to bet, but led by excitement, those who are willing to risk their money have *nerra dime* to venture with—while those who have money have become wise enough to keep it. The bar of the establishment, though adorned and arranged in the most tempting manner, has but few devotees. The thirst for gaming and drinking has undergone a greater change, perhaps, than any of the other evils to which California has been subjected.

Westward the Course of Empire

THE WAYFARER in California now finds every thing to make him comfortable which he will find in any other portion of the world. Splendid hotels, restaurants and boarding houses are to be met with at every turn. Board and lodging of the best and most comfortable kind can be had for from ten to fourteen dollars per week. Theatres, balls and concerts are to be enjoyed in every city and town.

The Sabbath day has had no change for the better from what it ever has been with us. Although the different churches are tolerably well attended, and the gaming tables closed in the fore part of the day; yet the sound of the church-going bell and the music to attract visitors to the ball and bear fights mingle together. The evenings of the day, consecrated in civilized communities to divine worship, are here spent in visiting the theatres, concerts and balls; the principal attractive features of which are kept for the Sunday evening's performances.

Although everything is here presented for man's happiness, there is a restless, unsettled, roving disposition alive within the community that cannot well be accounted for. For the want of a better name, I will call it "Madam Chivalry." When our flag was first unfurled as a fit emblem for the ancient fainting spirit of expiring chivalry to muster around, it was hailed by a fearless band, who swore not by the cross, but pledged themselves as a band of brothers to do battle in a modern crusade against the tyrants of earth, with human liberty as their shields—their helmets equal rights. From a little fearless band, there are now millions of knights who muster beneath the folds of this banner, which was first raised in the wilderness of a western world. The downtrodden of earth, whose hearts panted for freedom, hastened to it, and swore eternal allegiance to its cause. From the shores of the Atlantic to where Pacific's waves wash the strand, it has been unfurled on every height—its watch-fires burn upon every hill-top—the valleys send forth their songs of gladness from the feasts of the "harvest home," while the goddess of liberty sits smiling upon her sons.

America, great and free,
A world now turns to thee
And asks thee, as once of Rome,
Give us justice and a home.

There is now a spirit alive in California, which may be good or it may be fraught with evil, but time will tell. The ever restless, adventurous and daring spirit that constitutes the most prominent feature in the dispositions of the American people is here fully developed. Let a call be made for volunteers in an Indian war, or by the weak powers of a Central American state, and gold at once loses its attraction for our people; a rush is made by them for their ever ready arms, in hopes of enjoying the *pleasures* of war. 'Tis folly to think that the star of empire has set on the shores of the Pacific—it will still "Westward take its way."

VIII. Thou shalt not steal a pick, or a shovel, or a pan from thy fellow miner; nor take away his tools without his leave; nor borrow those he cannot spare; nor return them broken, nor trouble him to fetch them back again, nor talk with him while his water rent is running on, nor remove his stake to enlarge thy claim, nor undermine his bank in following a lead, nor pan out gold from his "riffle box," nor wash the "tailings" from his sluice's mouth. Neither shalt thou pick out specimens from the company's pan to put them in thy mouth, or in thy purse; nor cheat thy partner of his share; nor steal from thy cabin-mate his gold dust, to add to thine, for he will be sure to discover what thou hast done, and will straightaway call his fellow miners together, and if the law hinder them not, they will hang thee, or give thee fifty lashes, or shave thy head and brand thee, like a horse thief, with "R" upon thy cheek, to be known and read of all men, Californians in particular. (James M. Hutchings, *The Miners' Ten Commandments*.)

If the U.S. has any particular business to attend to in the islands of the Pacific, or wish to see how our pretty flag would look while flying over the Sandwich or Japanese Islands, just let Uncle Sam call on California for a few able bodied, free white citizens, between the ages of eighteen and forty-five years, and in ten days we will furnish the old gentleman with ten thousand of the sweetest specimens of humanity for a little job of that kind the world ever saw.

Deeds of murder, and quick executions for that crime and for theft, are still the order of the day. The newspapers have one or more of these to detail at every issue—blackening their pages in the eyes of the world. The press in California has to be conducted on the *fast* principle, to be the leaders in our progression. In detailing murders and public executions, the facts are stated in as few words as possible. For instance: two or three men are murdered and robbed; the occurrence would be noted in the daily papers by saying—

"Three men were brutally murdered in their tent, near —— diggings, and robbed of a large amount of gold known to be in their possession. The miners in the vicinity followed the perpetrators of the deed, and took them at ——, and brought them back; a jury was formed by the people, who tried the culprits, found them guilty, and sentenced them to be hung in an hour afterwards, which execution took place at — o'clock, on the evening of the ——."

We take up a paper printed in the Eastern States, and any other *slow* place in such matters, and we there see five or six columns devoted to the details of such an occurrence, stating the full particulars, with a printed diagram of the place the murder occurred, the personal appearance of the deceased, how they lay, looked, felt and smelt on the occasion, and in probably six months after the murderers have been taken, the press for a week will be engaged in giving the full details of their trials; if a conviction can be had for the deed, the poor devils are tortured another month by the long faces of psalm singers, feelers of their phrenological bumps, and pointed and levelled at by the tubes of the practitioners of the Daguerrean art, and then scientifically hung. The hanging affords the press another chance for its descriptive powers, in detailing the full circumstances, how the *hombres* acted, their last words and actions, and even which foot he last kicked with will be given in the solemn detail. Such descriptions as these are too *slow* for our California press, and another

VI. Thou shalt not kill thy body by working in the rain, even
though thou shalt make enough to buy physic and attendance
with. Neither shalt thou kill thy neighbor's body in a duel; for
by "keeping cool," thou canst save his life and thy conscience.
Neither shalt thy destroy thyself by getting "tight," nor
"stewed," nor "high," nor "corned," nor "half-seas over," nor
"three sheets in the wind," by drinking smoothly down
—"brandy slings," "gin cocktails," "whisky punches," "rum-
toddies," nor "egg nogs." Neither shalt thou suck "mint-
julips," nor "sherry-cobblers," through a straw, nor gurgle
from a bottle the "raw material," nor "take it neat" from a
decanter; for, while thou art swallowing down thy purse, and
thy coat from off thy back, thou art burning the coat from off
thy stomach; and, if thou couldst see the houses and lands, and
gold dust, and home comforts already lying there—"a huge
pile"—thou shouldst feel a choking in thy throat; and when to
that thou addest thy crooked walkings and hiccuping talkings,
of lodgings in the gutter, of broilings in the sun, of prospect-
holes half full of water, and of shafts and ditches, from which
thou hast emerged like a drowning rat, thou wilt feel disgusted with thyself, and inquire, "Is thy servant a dog that he
doeth these things?" verily I will say, Farewell, old bottle, I
will kiss thy gurgling lips no more. And thou, slings, cocktails,
punches, smashes, cobblers, nogs, toddies, sangarees, and
julips, forever farewell. Thy remembrance shames me; hence-
forth, "I cut thy acquaintance," and headaches, tremblings,
heart burnings, blue devils, and all the unholy catalogue of
evils that follow in thy train. My wife's smiles and my
children's merry-hearted laugh, shall charm and reward me
for having the manly firmness and courage to say *NO*.
I wish thee an eternal farewell.
(James M. Hutchings, *The Miners' Ten Commandments*.)

thing, our editors know that such articles in their columns would not be entertaining to their readers.

Our community at the present time has not that pure, industrious, business face on it that it once had; refinement seems to be corrupting it. In 1848, '49 and '50, every man was in employment or business of some kind, but we now see hundreds of idlers in our community, who go well dressed, loafing from one place to another, and are destitute of that necessary appendage called money—how do they live? Others, great hearty men are to be seen organ-grinding, peddling, and hawking around hot pies, segars and pop corn, the percentage of which would not pay the whisky they drink, and this too in a country like California, where the poorest laborer on a farm can get $75 per month, or $150 per month, and found, in the mines. These drones of society must live, and how they can here get along as they do, is only known to themselves. There is another class to be met with in California who should long ago have been put under the kind protection of Judge Lynch. I mean the sleek faced swindlers, that have, and now are making fortunes out of the California gold mines without ever touching the handle of a pick. If a poor devil steals an old mule worth twenty dollars, we hang him for it, but if a villain swindles individuals out of thousands of dollars there is no exertion made to bring him to punishment for it. Meeting an old acquaintance, with whom I wintered in the mines in 1849, inquiry passed between us concerning those who were then our companions. One in particular who always had a perfect disrespect for gold digging, I asked my friend about; in what manner he lived, and where he was? he informed me that Mr. —— had gone home with a pile. "You know," says he, "that he would never work, and he came here to get gold, and he done it by settling down and making out legal papers necessary for an immense mining company, had the names of a President, Secretary, and a full Board of Directors to it, and his own name attached as sole agent for the company. Thus armed and equipped he went south to sell shares. The rich specimens of gold bearing quartz he had in his possession, were shown to those athirst for stock, that was warranted to yield at least one hundred per cent, as an average of the company's rich vein. Fifty per cent was to be paid when the stock was taken, and but a short time elapsed before Mr. —— had realized fifty thousand dollars by the operation, and left for parts unknown. How many other gentlemen of this class have made fortunes in the same way? Let our own people, and good *merrie* Old England, who have been bled with quartz rock to the tune of millions of dollars answer the question.

How many of our honest unsuspicious miners have been swindled out of all their hard earnings, in inconceivable ways by this same class, and the villains are revelling on the spoils. How is it that these rascals have escaped punishment? Judge Lynch should be impeached for the neglect. In regard to California mining companies, the utmost caution should be used. There are millions of dollars in the quartz mines of California that can be got with proper means. There are now companies who are realising two hundred per cent on their investments, which can be doubled by proper means. Others, with the inadequate machinery employed, are not paying their expenses, while scores of them have failed. It requires capital to develop this the richest mineral resources of the state, and one that will give such dividends on capital invested as to make speculators greedily invest money in any thing like a quartz mining company. This circumstance is known by the swindlers and sharpers who have deluded, blinded and swindled even the smartest and most careful business men, by forming quartz companies for the purpose of making imaginary rich veins in imaginary places in California. Before shares are paid for or ever purchased, in any company got up for California, let the purchaser know positively that there is a paying vein of quartz well prospected, and that there is a sufficient claim warranted as the actual property of such company before he buys. Capitalists would have a much better chance to realise an income from investments in lottery tickets than they would from mining stock of California, now to be found in every market in the world.

My Heart has a Throb for Thee

A WORD TO THOSE WHO ARE HERE and those who wish to get here, and I will close. There is in a "Life in California," to those now here, a secret, glorious, independent recklessness which cannot be explained. We have everything around us to make man happy, a country on which nature has lavished her most precious gifts and blessed with a climate unequalled on earth. The only thing detrimental to our progression, is our legislation. We are yet young, and this can be improved by the people; but, thus far, civil government in California has been like a burlesque on an excellent play: where the people, as an audience, has paid dearly for a shadow of the substance. Our rulers fatten on the rich spoils of office, while anarchy is kept down by the "vigilance" of the people: a power we have, in the face of a civil government, to look to, for the protection of life and property. The great secret is that we have heretofore elected a majority of men to our legislatures, and to fill every office in the State, who have no earthly interest in California, or who do not design to remain here longer than is necessary to amass a fortune, and then quit the country forever. We have seen our model constitution trampled upon with impunity. It is too pure, too good for us, in the eyes of our wise lawgivers, and they want it altered, torn apart, so as to have it remodeled to suit their speculative schemes. In defiance of the people's wish, they have dared to ask it changed, and will no doubt use all the influence that money can give, to carry out their foul designs. The constitution of California is known to be one of the best for a free democratic government that has ever been framed. Those who framed and signed that pure instrument, did it for California, and not for individual designs; for they were men who had come to make this their home. But there are enough independent voters here to defeat the foul designs of speculators.

We now have the Foreign Miners' Tax, (once tried before,) again saddled upon us. Is unequal taxation constitutional in this State? Has the Legislature of California the power to enact any measure that will directly or indirectly prohibit an occupation of the public domain by honest, industrious emigrants from any part of the world? Are our relations with Asia to be improved by taxing its people distinctly and exorbitantly? We see our wise Government using every honorable means to open trade with China and the Asiatic Islands, which are to be the sources of California's commercial greatness; and instead of aiding these wise exertions to make California the great emporium of the commercial world, our "mutton-headed" State government has adopted one of the surest measures to prevent the consummation of this much desired object. Our school lands, the rich donation from a wise government, have been bartered away for State scrip; the lands given to our children will soon have passed into the hands of the moneyed monopoly at the low rate of two dollars per acre. When, now, will our ears be blessed with the hum of infant voices from the public schools? To perpetuate our ruin, sink us in a mass of crime, and cause streams of fraternal blood to flow across our fruitful fields, we have only to sink two generations in ignorance, and the end will be accomplished. Of what use is our glorious free press, if ignorance brutalizes the hearts and blinds the eyes of our people? There is now far sweeter music in the little newsboy's voice, to the ear of the republican, than that arising from a thousand armories of despotism. Every public school erected in our land is productive of more strength to our future greatness than a pillar of adamant. But in our State this has been overlooked. It is evident that a want of public schools in former years, is the secret influence which has initiated and passed so many ruinous measures through our Legislature.

To make fortunes out of the public, and create fat offices for favorites and idlers, appears to be the only aim of California Legislation. We have, for instance, a Superintendant of Public Buildings, who gets his thousands per annum—what does he do, of public utility? and to make fortunes for a few more favorites by a secret taxation, we have a Flour Inspector appointed and a Gauger and Inspector of Liquors whose offices will be paid from fifty to one hundred thousand dollars per annum, from the hard earnings of our people. Am I wrong in the face of this to say that the only thing to be feared in California Life, is its legislation? Such is legislation and such is "Life in California."

Of those who live in the Atlantic states, I would inquire: Have you a home? Have you a family? can you live independent of a master over you? If you have these, stay where you are. Have you to work hard for a living? Can you get six hundred dollars per year clear of expenses for your labor? Do you want a good farm to settle on? Do you want to live independent and happy, in one of the best climates in the world? If you do, come to California, *and make it your home*.

To those who are coming to this country for the purpose of making fortunes by swindling, robbery or theft, my parting advice to them, is, to *bring their coffins along*.

My thanks are due to a generous public for the kind reception these letters have met with. They have been written during the lucid hours of an invalid, for the purpose of making public, through the generosity of the *San Joaquin Republican*, many little incidents known to but few of the present inhabitants of California. The only thing to recommend them is, that they are *original facts*. The personal names of individuals in many of the scenes, can be given, but the great object of the writer was, to avoid everything that would create a frown from any of the actors.

I am one of those who have pitched their tents in California to remain in it forever—her interests are mine, and to thee, CALIFORNIA—

> My voice, though but *broken*, was raised for thy
>   light;
> My vote, as a Freeman, still voted thee free;
> This hand, though but feeble, would arm in thy
>   fight—
> And this heart, though outworn, has a throb
>   still for thee.

A report of the Tulare Valley

by Lieutenant George H. Derby

Major Canby's Orders to Lieutenant Derby

HEAD-QUARTERS 10TH MILITARY DEPARTMENT,
Monterey, California, April 9, 1850

Sir: The objects of the reconnoissance which you are about to make have already been verbally indicated to you, and I am now instructed by the commanding general to direct your attention again to the most important of these objects:

1st. An examination of the country between the latitude of San Miguel and that of San Luis Obispo, for the purpose of selecting a position that will cover the passes leading from the Tulare into the settled country east of San Luis Obispo.

2d. An examination of the passes between San Miguel and Santa Margarita, and of the valley of the Tulare from that neighborhood to the King's river, for the purpose of ascertaining whether there is a practicable route for loaded wagons from the coast to King's river.[1]

---

1. See the footnote on page 16.

This route should cross the Sanjon de San José[2] at or near its junction with the lake; and it is important to ascertain whether any portion of this route is overflown in the seasons of high water. If so, what portion of it, and for what period of the year. The route from San Luis Obispo has already been examined by Captain Warner,[3] and it will only be necessary to examine that portion of it that lies east of the San Luis and Monterey Road.

If, however, you should have time, it will be well to ascertain the present condition of the road from San Luis to Santa Margarita, and also whether the land transportation may not be diminished by landing supplies at Estero bay, instead of the Bay of San Luis. Captain John Wilson[4] is suggested to you as a person from whom you may obtain much reliable information in relation to this subject, as well, also, as to the safety of Estero bay for vessels. If you should visit Estero bay, the latitude and longitude of the Moro will be determined.

3d. The examination of the country on the eastern side of the Tulare from the San Joaquin river on the north to the latitude of ——— on the south, for the purpose of selecting a suitable position for the establishment of a military post in the neighborhood of the Tulare lake.

The objects to be attained in making this establishment, will be the protection of the frontier east of San Luis Obispo from Indian excursions, and the control of the Indians inhabiting the borders of the lakes and the slopes of the Sierra Nevada, east and north of those lakes. The No-tonto[5] village occupies a central position for these purposes, and has heretofore been suggested as a suitable

---

2. Now known as Fresno Slough, the erstwhile waterway that connected the San Joaquin River with Taché Lake (Tulare Lake).
3. Lieutenant William Horace Warner of the topographical engineers was with Stephen W. Kearny's Army of the West. He was wounded at the battle of San Pasqual on December 6, 1846; the site of the battle is east of the present city of Escondido. Warner was killed by Indians on September 26, 1849, in northern California. The Warner Mountains are named for him.
4. John Wilson, a Scots shipmaster and trader, first came to California in 1826 on the English ship *Thomas Nowlan*. Before 1836 he married Ramona Carrillo de Pacheco, the widow of the elder Romualdo Pacheco and the mother of Governor Pacheco. In 1845 Wilson and James Scott purchased the San Luis Obispo estate. Wilson was granted the ranchos Cañada del Chorro and Cañada de los Osos. He lived on the latter until his death in 1860.
5. See footnote 1 on page 75.

position for the establishment of a military post. You will give a particular attention to the examination of points in that neighborhood, indicating the several points that may possess the necessary requisites for military posts, and reporting particularly for the information of the brigadier-general commanding; the comparative advantages of each; the military and general resources of the country in the neighborhood; the facility with which lateral communication may be made for the purpose of operating against the Indians of that country, and the nature and length of the route by which the command to be stationed there must be supplied. Particular attention will also be given to the collection of such information as may be useful in guarding against the selection of an unhealthy position; and among other facts, you will ascertain, if practicable, the direction of the prevalent winds during the summer and fall months, and the nature of the country (whether marshy or otherwise) over which they pass.

4th. The selection of the route by which supplies are to be sent from the coast being of very great importance, you will bestow particular care in the examination of such as may be discovered by or suggested to you. In addition to that already indicated to you, there are two others to which your attention will be directed. The first of these is from the highest point of navigation on the San Joaquin by the valley of that river to the neighborhood of the point at which the post is to be established. The second is from Monterey by some practicable pass in the coast range, if one can be discovered, to the neighborhood of the same point.

Both of these routes will probably cross the Sanjon de San José at its junction with the San Joaquin river, and be the same for the remainder of the distance. For the first of these routes it will only be necessary to ascertain the point to which vessels may ascend the San Joaquin, and the length and nature of the road from that point to the crossing of the San Joaquin or the Sanjon, as the case may be; and for the second examination of such of the passes in the coast range between Pancheca's [Pacheco's] and San Miguel as may promise to be practicable for loaded wagons.

Care will be taken to select for the passage of any streams that it may be necessary to cross, points at which the banks on both sides are accessible by wagons at all seasons of the year, that the length of the different routes should be ascertained, and that the nature of any obstacles should be fully reported.

In addition to the above you are desired to collect and report, for the information of the commanding general, any reliable information in relation to the general and military resources of the country through which you pass; its geological structure, &c.; &c.; and to determine as accurately as your means will permit, the latitude and longitude of the northern extremities of the lakes Tache and Buena Vista, and any other important points.

The infantry company under the command of Lieutenant Moore[6] is designed to cover your operations while engaged in the Indian country in the vicinity of the Tulare, and that officer will be instructed to do this effectually, and to render you any assistance that may be needed. For the ordinary purposes of assistance and protection in the performance of your duties, the topographical party hereto-fore authorized (one guide and eight men) will be sufficient, if your operations are conducted within a reasonable distance of that command. If, however, that force at any time be found insufficient, you will make requisitions upon Lieutenant Moore for any escort that may be deemed necessary.

The commanding general does not anticipate any difficulties with the Indians that you may encounter in your operations, but it will be necessary to be constantly on the guard, and that you should not at any time place yourself beyond the reach of assistance. You will see that the Indians whom you meet are treated kindly by your party, but you will not suffer them to remain in large parties about your camp. The utmost economy will be observed in your operations; and the commanding general directs that no expenditures be made, or obligations contracted, except such as are indispensably necessary.

Very respectfully your obedient servant.

ED. R. S. CANBY,
Assistant Adjutant General.

---

6. Lieutenant Tredwell Moore of the U.S. Army served in the San Joaquin Valley and in the Sierra Nevada for several years. In 1852, while leading troops in pursuit of Indians who had killed two white prospectors in Yosemite Valley in May of that year, he crossed Mono Pass to the east side of the Sierra. He named the pass and discovered and named Mono Lake.

Lieutenant Derby's Report

MONTEREY, *July 10, 1850.*

Major: I have the honor to report that in compliance with the above instructions, I left for Monterey upon the 10th of April, with my party and the escort assigned for the duty, and proceeded at once to the completion of the duties assigned to me in articles one and two, which occupied me until the 26th, when I returned to San Miguel and reported to you in detail the result of my operations. In the discharge of these duties I measured and took the bearings of the road from Monterey to San Luis Obispo, observing also the latitude and longitude of the principal intermediate points, (a summary of which will be found in the margin,) and I examined thoroughly the ranges of the coast mountains to the east of the road, for the purpose of ascertaining if there could be any communication with the sea from a point between San Miguel and San Luis Obispo.

The road from San Miguel to San Luis Obispo, I found generally good; between Passo de Roblas (a rancho upon the road about fifteen miles from San Miguel and Santa Margarita,) there are two or three places, however, where for a short distance the ground is constantly muddy, and there is a long and somewhat steep hill to be surmounted three miles west of San Luis Obispo, but these are difficulties of no particular importance, and the road may be, and is in fact at present, constantly travelled by vehicles of every description. The bay of San Simeon, in latitude 35° 40′ north, is in appearance, a good roadstead, and is well protected from the north and west; but I was informed that both this and Estero bay, which is an indentation in the coast in latitude 35° 20′ north, (nine miles north of San Luis Obispo,) are impracticable for anything but the smaller class of vessels, drawing but about eight or ten feet of water, and their entrances dangerous, and obstructed by rocks and sand-bars.

The bay of San Luis Obispo, on the contrary, I found highly recommended as easy of entrance, safe and commodious; but as I was obliged to obtain my information from residents of that place, which, with its few half ruined adobe buildings, they persist in considering a thriving city, I think it possible their opinions on the subject may be

Lieutenant George Horatio Derby. The drawing was made from a photograph.
It appeared in the *San Francisco Chronicle* on October 24, 1897 in an article
on early California writers.

slightly prejudicial. The bay appears well, however, and is certainly sufficiently extensive. I observed a large brig lying at anchor inside, while there. As I had no instructions to that effect, and it would have occupied some time, I made no particular examination of these bays, or the intermediate coast, but I would respectfully suggest the propriety of having a general survey made of the bay of San Simeon, as the several opinions to which I listened on the subject I found materially conflicting. Between the valley of Santa Margarita and the coast, a distance of about twenty-one miles, there are two distinct ranges of mountains, which we examined north and south, for fifteen miles. They are steep, rocky and barren, or covered with shrubs, and no pass can be found through or over them to the coast, south of Santa Margarita.

From Paso de Roblas, however, I discovered a horse trail running almost due west, which, although it crosses two very declivitous hills and is seldom travelled, may, I think, be made a wagon road to San Simeon bay, should that be found of importance. At present, the residents of the ranchos in the vicinity of San Simeon and Estero bays, in travelling to Monterey, take the beach around by San Luis Obispo, and they appeared much surprised that we had succeeded in getting our mules over the mountains at all. We found but three passes through the coast range to the west of the road between the latitude of San Miguel and that of San Luis. These are the two roads, the one from San Miguel, the other from San Luis, (via Paso de Roblas,) which, meeting at a point called Estrella, form the pass of San Miguel; and a road passing through a cañada in the hills about fifteen miles east of San Luis, called the Penoche Pass,[7] which debouches near the head of Buena Vista Lake, and might with a little labor be made an excellent wagon path. This last, in the event of San Luis becoming a large seaport and the probable discovery of rich mines upon the streams of the Tulare valley, may become of great importance.

Having finished my examination and obtained what information I could with regard to the Tulare valley, I returned with my party to the infantry encampments upon the 26th. We left San Miguel on the 28th, and crossing the river within three hundred yards of the

---

7. This name is not on present maps. It probably is Pozo Summit.

Misión San Miguel Arcángel—San Miguel Mission. Drawing by Edward Vischer, 1864. An additional caption by Vischer read: "Sheriff and Posse conducting a band of criminals towards San Luis Obispo."

mission, proceeded up a deep ravine in the hills through which we found a trail leading out upon the banks of a small stream, at a distance of two miles from the river. This stream has its rise near the summit of this portion of the range; it is about eighteen miles in length, and flowing in a south-west direction,[8] empties into the Monterey river[9] about a mile above the mission; with the exception of two or three springs in its bed, it is dry during the summer, and its valley forms the western portion of the pass; keeping the bank of the stream, we passed through a beautiful and fertile valley over an excellent road, arriving at Estrella early in the afternoon.[10] The distance of this point from San Miguel we found by the viameter to be 12.77 miles;[11] it is a beautiful spot covered with fine large oaks, and with a little cultivation the soil might be rendered extremely productive. There is a never failing spring of water near the bank of the creek, which we discovered and enlarged. Four valleys diverge from this point, through the south-west one of which leads the road from San Louis Obispo, entering from the main coast road near the rancho "Paso de Roblas." The peculiarity of the divergence of these four valleys, and their corresponding ridges from this point resembling the rays of a star, has given it its very appropriate name—Estrella. We encamped here on the 28th, and leaving early the next morning proceeded through the pass, having previously sent forward a party of pioneers to make any repairs upon the road that might be found necessary. Keeping the valley of the stream for about six miles, bearing about east by north, we struck a narrow valley or cañada, through which we passed and emerged, after travelling about eleven miles, upon a plain about six miles in length by one or two in width.[12] Crossing this plain, and still continuing to follow the course of the stream, we encamped about two p.m. at its source, a point about two

---

8. Derby apparently made a simple mistake in writing his report. The Estrella River flows west-northwest.
9. The Salinas River.
10. Not the place presently named Estrella, but rather about seven miles southeast, where state route 46 crosses the Estrella River.
11. A viameter was a wheel that was pulled behind a cart or wagon. It had a clockwork device that recorded the number of revolutions of the wheel and thus the number of miles traveled. Other words for the same thing are 'cyclometer' and 'hodometer.'
12. Cholame Valley.

miles from the summit of the range, and distant 16.83 miles by the
viameter from Estrella. The road we found excellent, no repairs
being required, the country barren, but little grass and a few stunted
trees and shrubs growing on the margin of the stream. We observed
many antelopes feeding in the cañadas upon our right and left, and
killed a large rattlesnake while on the road. Near our encampment
three distinct ridges of trap rock, about half a mile a part, run north
and south through the hills as far as the eye can reach, presenting
precisely the appearance of foundations of ruined walls. They vary in
height from six inches to twenty feet, and are about six feet in thickness, but the most singular circumstance connected with them is
the fact, *that they lie as nearly as possible in the plane of the true
meridian.* We had found at San Miguel, by observation, the magnetic
variations to be 15° 28′ east, and we now found the bearing of these
ridges by the compass N. 15° 30′ W. On the 30th we crossed the dividing ridge[13] without difficulty, and arriving at a spring about five
miles from the summit concluded to encamp, although we had made
but six and three quarter miles by the viameter, as I feared we
should find no more water until our arrival at the lake, which I
thought at too great a distance for one day's march. The road we
found very tolerable, but requiring some little repair, as the trail lay
upon the side of the hills, which in some places are quite steep. Upon
the whole I have no hesitation in saying that the road through the
pass is quite as good, and needs as little repair as any portion of the
road between Monterey and San Miguel of the same length, and is by
far the best pass through the coast range of mountains not excepting
Livermore's. Crossing a plain 6.04 miles by the viameter in width,
upon the 1st of May we came to a small stream called *Dick's creek,*[14]
which, rising in the hills, flows south for about twelve miles, and
loses itself in the sandy soil, forming during the rainy season quite
an extensive marsh at its termination. Here we found good water,
and the banks of the creek lined with wild oats, affording excellent
grazing for the animals; I concluded therefore to encamp here, and
proceed with my party to examine the trail leading in the direction

13. Cottonwood Summit on state route 41.
14. Probably Avenal Creek.

of the lake, which I hoped to be able to reach and return from before sundown.

The escort having arrived and encamped in our vicinity, I started accordingly at about 10 a.m., and, crossing two ranges of low hills over a broad and smooth trail, arrived on the shore of the great Taché lake[15] about 1 p.m. We were unable to get close to the water, in consequence of the tulé which environed it extending into the lake from two hundred yards to one-fourth of a mile, as far as the eye could reach. With a glass I could distinguish the timber at the north and the tulé at the south ends of the lake, the length of which I estimated at about twenty miles, but we could not distinctly make out the opposite or eastern shore. The peaks of the Sierra Nevada, at this place twelve thousand feet above the level of the sea and covered with perpetual snow, appeared in close proximity, and, rising far above the horizon, seemed to us to come down precipitously to the very edge of the water. The distance from our encampment to the lake we estimated at eighteen miles, or nearly a day's march, and as the country passed over was a perfect desert, and I found here no forage for the animals but wire grass, the water standing in the tulé marshes blackish, and no wood at all, I concluded to return immediately to camp, and in the morning to make a reconnoissance to the south of our position, for the purpose of finding a road to the southern extremity of the lake, which point I hoped to be able to reach in one day's march. An examination was accordingly made on the 2d, (a portion of the party being left in camp to cut wild oats, which I purposed to transport for forage, as it was evident we would find none upon the shores of the lake,) which terminated favorably, a good path being found through the southern extremity of the valley, and a trail leading apparently around the south of the lake. On the 3d we broke up our pleasant encampment at *Dick's creek,* and succeeded in reaching the southern part of the lake, where we encamped upon the sand for the night, having marched twenty-four and a quarter miles nearly in an easterly direction from the termination of the pass. We found here a ridge of sand about one hundred yards in width, and twelve feet above the level of the lake, which divides the water of the

---

15. Tulare Lake, now entirely gone. See the map.

northern or Taché from the bed (now nearly dry,) of the southern or
Ton Taché lake. This last is little more than a very extensive swamp,
covering the plain for fifteen miles in a southerly direction, and is
about ten in width. It is filled with sloughs and small tulé lakes, and
is of course impassable, except with the assistance of boats or rafts.
The gradual receding of the water is distinctly marked by the ridges
of decayed tulé upon its shore, and I was informed, and see no reason
to disbelieve, that ten years ago it was nearly as extensive a sheet of
water as the northern lake, having been gradually drained by the connecting sloughs, and its bed filled by the encroachments of the tulé.
We crossed the slough on the 4th, being assisted with rafts of tulé by
the rancheria of *Sin Taché*[16] Indians, which we found established at
this point. They were about one hundred in number, mostly clothed,
and very friendly. The captain was an old Indian from the San Luis
Obispo mission, and spoke Spanish indifferently well. Several of
these Indians had bits of paper on which were written recommenda-
tions, signed by various persons, Spanish and American, by which
they set great store, and eagerly exhibited for our examination.

I gave the captain a certificate that he had treated us kindly, and
proceeding on over the desert, which we found very painful travelling for the animals, encamped on the southeast point of the lake,
having made 12.64 miles. We found here another small rancheria
called the Tinte Tachés,[17] living, like the others, principally on fish
and reptiles, and numbering about fifty. I had a conversation with the
captain, who was quite an intelligent old fellow, originally belonging
to the mission of San Miguel. He informed me that the Taché Indians,
of which tribe his rancheria formed a portion, numbered about eight
hundred in all, and were settled on the shores of the great lake, but
their principal rancheria, containing about three hundred, is situated
at its northwest extremity. They are all peaceable and friendly in
their dispositions; and he assured me that they had never stolen or
eaten horseflesh, which, judging from the meagre condition of himself and companions, I should think highly probable. We gave them

16. Derby confused the Tachi Indians with the Chunut; these are now thought to have
been Chunut. The Tachi lived north of Tulare Lake. Derby at this point is at the
southern end of that lake.
17. Probably Wowol, the third tribe that inhabited the shores of Tulare Lake.

some bread and a little sugar, with which they were highly gratified, and in the morning brought us some dried fish in return, which we accepted, but could make no use of. On the 5th, after marching 15.38 miles over a continuation of the barren sandy desert which had been our route for the last three days, we came to two or three cottonwood trees upon a small stream called Moore's creek,[18] which empties near this point into the Ton Taché swamp, and here, the grass being very tolerable, we encamped. This is the first point on our route where good water, grass, or wood is to be found after leaving Dick's creek. It will therefore be seen that it is necessary for loaded wagons to transport, if travelling this route, sufficient grain to forage their teams for three days.

As I deemed it unnecessary for the infantry escort to accompany me through the desert to Buena Vista lake, which it now became necessary to examine, I proceeded up Moore's creek on the 6th for 12.20 miles, to a point about five miles west of the high peaks of the Sierra Nevada, where I found an excellent encampment, the creek at this point, and above among the hills, being lined with cottonwood and willows and some large oaks, the grass among which was growing luxuriously. Here Lieutenant Moore encamped his party to await my return from the Buena Vista lake, an examination of the country in the vicinity of which I thought might take five or six days.

On the 7th, taking my party, I ascended Moore's creek for about twenty miles among the hills, and found it a small rapid stream, about fifty feet wide, the water extremely cold from the melting of the snow upon the Sierra, and about two feet in depth. We discovered two small branches, upon each of which we observed the ruined remains of a large rancheria. The banks of the stream, as well as the hills surrounding, were heavily timbered with oaks, and three large species of pine.

Leaving Moore's creek we crossed through the ravines in the mountains to Tulé river, which runs in the same direction as the former stream, (a little north of east,) and at about eight or ten miles north of it, emptying into the southeastern extremity of the Taché lake. This stream has two branches, the upper portion of which is

---

18. Present-day Deer Creek. See footnote 4 on page 62.

well timbered, but the banks are swampy near the lake, and for a
long distance in the plain, the Tulé running up to within five miles
of the hills. At this time the stream was about a hundred yards wide,
from twelve to twenty feet deep, and very rapid, which last is a general characteristic of all the streams to the east of the lake. Upon its
upper banks and their vicinity in the hills, plenty of large pines are
found; lower down it is well timbered with the different species of
oak, sycamore, cottonwood, and willow.

Ascending the stream about ten miles, we suddenly came upon a
rancheria of Indians in a sequestered nook of the hills. We swam the
river and were met upon the bank by all the men (sixty or seventy)
belonging to the band. They received us favorably, although with evident distrust, and informed us that they belonged to the *Thulimé*[19]
tribe. I had been previously told by the captain of the Ton Tachés
that they were a hostile, thieving nation, and observed about their
rancheria several horses and skeletons of animals, the appearance of
which was calculated to corroborate this information. I directed the
interpreter to state to them, that while they conducted themselves
properly they would be treated with kindness and consideration, but
that if detected in horse-stealing or other crimes against the whites,
they would be sure to meet with the severest punishment; and that
for the purpose of protecting their interests, as well as its own, the
government was about to establish a post, and send soldiers to reside
in their vicinity. They appeared to understand this perfectly; but I
am inclined to think it made but little impression upon them, and I
was unable to obtain from any of them the name of their captain, or
the entire number of the tribe. After remaining about an hour at the
rancheria we returned to camp, having asked two or three who spoke
Spanish to accompany us, which invitation they declined. I suspected
that nothing but our numbers and the well-armed condition of the
party prevented our being treated with incivility.

We left Lieutenant Moore's encampment early on the 8th, taking
with us but one pack-mule and the cart, which was necessary on account of the attached viameter, and proceeding S.S.W. thirty-four

---

19. The Telamni tribe.

miles, encamped upon a small stream called Cottonwood creek,[20] having crossed early in the day, at a distance of eight miles from Moore's encampment, another small stream which I called Gopher creek.[21] The latter, I think, is dry during the summer months, but the former is undoubtedly constant during the year. Our route this day was over the most miserable country that I ever beheld. The soil was not only of the most wretched description, dry, powdery and decomposed, but was everywhere burrowed by gophers, and a small animal resembling a common house-rat, which I had never seen before, of a whitish grey color, short round body, and very strong bony head. These animals are innumerable; though what they subsist upon I cannot conceive, for there was little or no vegetation. Their holes and burrows, into which a horse sinks to his knees at almost every step, render their travelling difficult and dangerous. The low hills south of Gopher creek extend about eight miles into the plain, their summit being about on the same level as the plain between that stream and Moore's creek, and are singularly intersected by valleys running nearly south and north, which are crossed by other numerous small valleys running nearly east and west, thus dividing the whole of this portion of the valley into blocks of hills about a quarter of a mile square, and from one hundred to three hundred feet in height. In riding through these valleys the country presents the appearance of a large city which has been partially overwhelmed by the ashes of volcanic eruptions, which resemblance is heightened by the continual cropping out of upright strata of clay from the loose soil of the hills, resembling exactly the ruined walls of adobe houses.

On the 9th we arrived, after a march of thirteen miles, upon the north bank of the Kern river, a very broad and deep stream with a current of six miles an hour, which, rising high up in the Sierra Nevada, discharges itself by two mouths into Buena Vista lake near its northern extremity. Three large sloughs also make out from the river near its mouth and form an extensive swamp in the plain upon the north bank of the lake. We found the river impassable with animals, and had not time to make a sufficient raft, I therefore

---

20. Poso Creek, probably the stream that Garcés called *Rio de Santiago* in 1776.
21. White River.

concluded to examine its northern bank on the tenth, and proceed to the northern extremity of the lake for the purpose of ascertaining its latitude and longitude, as well as its general character and appearance.

Buena Vista lake is a sheet of water about ten miles in length and from four to six miles in width; it lies about eight miles from the head of the valley formed by the junction of the ridges of the coast range and Sierra Nevada. Like the other bodies of water in the valley it is nearly surrounded with tulé, and upon its north and east banks there is found a heavy growth of willows. A slough some sixty miles in length, connects it with the swamps and bodies of standing water in the bed of the Ton Taché, and through them with the great northern lake. The surrounding country is sterile and unproductive when not an absolute swamp, with the exception of that portion lying immediately at the head of the valley, and among the ridges of the surrounding hills, where are some extremely fertile and well timbered spots, two of which are now occupied and cultivated as ranches or farms. Nothing can be conceived more inappropriate than its name, for no place can be imagined more forlorn or desolate in aspect.[22] Even at the early season of our visit, clouds of the most venomous musquitoes tormented us during the day, and goaded us to madness during the night; and we found here scorpions, centipedes, and a small but extremely poisonous rattlesnake about eighteen inches in length, reptiles which we had not before noticed in the valley, and which with the gophers and ground rats are the only denizens of this unpleasant and uninhabited spot. A road from Los Angelos, passing through what is called the Tejon, at the head of the valley, crosses Kern river about thirteen miles above its junction with the lake, and continues through the valley to the eastward of the lakes, as far north as the mining district upon the Stanislaus river. On the 11th we started on

---

22. In 1772 Pedro Fages referred to an Indian village on the lake's shore that he called "Buena Vista."

"It should be remembered that the dry and arid plains of modern Kings, Tulare, and Kern counties bear no resemblance to the former region of rivers, sloughs, swamps, and lakes which once supported uncounted millions of game birds and animals, together with a luxurious vegetation capable of supporting a very dense human population." (S. F. Cook.)

our return to Moore's creek, taking a path about fifteen miles west of what we had followed in leaving, for the purpose of more thoroughly examining the country. We found it, however, of precisely the same character throughout—barren, decomposed soil, and no trace of vegetation but a few straggling artemisias, except upon the margin of the creeks. Gopher creek we found entirely dry at the point of crossing, its shallow stream sinking in the sandy soil some eight or ten miles above. We reached Lieutenant Moore's encampment about four o'clock p.m., on the 12th, somewhat fatigued and excessively hungry after our disagreeable march; for in the hurry of leaving our pork and coffee had been forgotten, and as we had seen no game upon the road, we were obliged for four days to subsist entirely upon the hard bread, with which, reduced to a fine powder by its jolting on the mule, we made with water a species of poultice, which had served as an indifferent palliative to the cravings of our appetites.

We immediately set about making preparations for our march to the north, and having no reason to apprehend danger from the Indians, I concluded to take but six of Lieutenant Moore's command with me as an escort, and those but to King river, intending to dispense with the services of the escort entirely from that point. But on arriving at Tulé river, which, at the point of crossing we found on the 13th to be but 7.16 miles from Moore's creek, I met a Mr. Shumway, who, with a single Indian, was travelling south to establish a ferry upon Kern river, and he informed me that there was not the slightest danger to be apprehended upon the route, the Indians being all friendly; he, with a single companion, having travelled through them from the Mariposa river, I deemed it unnecessary to require the services of an escort beyond this point. Accordingly, after sending back to the encampments for the wagon floats, which were required in crossing the river, being here about one hundred and fifty feet in width and extremely rapid, and getting my party safely upon the northern bank, Lieutenant Moore returned with his party to their encampment and took up their line of march for Monterey. The country had improved much in aspect from the time of leaving Moore's creek, and upon Tulé river; and during our march upon the 14th, we passed over rich tracts of arable land, fertile with every description of grass, and covered in many places with a fine growth of heavy oak timber. I observed that Tulé river might be

easily bridged, it being then at its highest stage and not subject to
overflow, and upon its banks could be found plenty of timber available for the purpose, while the rocky hills about five miles above the
crossing would furnish stone for the abutments and a pier, which
last could be erected upon a small island of hard gravel, covered at
present with willows, and situated at this point near the middle of
the stream. Upon the 14th we arrived at the river Frances,[23] a large
stream nineteen miles to the north of the Tulé. This stream flows
nearly west from the hills and empties into the Taché lake about
twenty miles north of its south-eastern extremity. It is, at the point
upon which we arrived, divided into five branches or sloughs, four of
which separate from the main river, about five miles above, joining
again from one to ten miles below, while the southern branch has
a separate and distinct course from the Sierra, and joins the main
stream in the marshy ground near its junction with the lake. The
country, eight miles in length by six in width, contained between
these branches, is a beautiful, smooth, level plain, covered with
clover of different kinds and high grass, and thickly shaded by one
continuous grove of oaks of a larger and finer description than any
I have seen in the country.

At this time each of the creeks was at its height; they are deep
and rapid, and four of them much wider than the Tulé river. Their
beds were also obstructed with floating and sunken timber previously felled for bridges, which the high stage of the water rendered useless; and we would have found it difficult to cross had it not been for
the kind assistance of the neighboring Indians who flocked to meet
us, and eagerly went to work carrying instruments and other property upon their heads, and swimming the animals and the little cart
across without the slightest accident occurring.

These poor people accompanied us from creek to creek, assisting
us cheerfully at each crossing, and in return for their kindness I gave
them a portion of our provisions and some dirty shirts, stockings and
worn-out boots which they prized as articles of exceeding luxury,
and accepted with vast satisfaction. There are two large rancherias
on the river numbering together about four hundred; they are, how-

23. The Kaweah River. See the footnote on page 59.

ever, apparently quite separate and distinct, one occupying the three southern, the other the two northern branches. Nothing could exceed the kindness and hospitality with which they treated us, and I gave the captain certificates to that effect, which they will undoubtedly present to all future passers by. The name of the first rancheria, as nearly as I could write it from their pronunciation, is He-ame-e-tahs;[24] their captain, De-e-jah. The second rancheria is the Cowees;[25] their captain, Francisco, an old mission Indian from San Luis Obispo. They called the river Ee-dek, but I think the name of Frances much more euphonious. There were many mission Indians among them, some from the old mission of San Juan, some from San Lorenzo, but mostly from San Miguel and San Luis Obispo. All these spoke Spanish a little. They appeared remarkably healthy, and though by no means beautiful, were comparatively well favored. The soil between the creeks being so well watered and shaded, is naturally of the richest description; as an evidence of which I may mention that I observed poles of willow stuck in the ground by Indians as parts of rabbit traps, which had taken root and sprouted into trees. The distance of the first or *Pyramid* creek (so called from the remarkable shape of a hill near which it rises) to the second is ninety-eight hundredths of a mile; from the second to the third, one mile; between the third and fourth, the last of which is the main stream, 2.81 miles, and between the fourth and fifth, eighty-five hundredths of a mile.

The third, or main stream, and the fourth are the widest and most difficult of crossing; the second and fifth I believe to be dry during the summer, but they may all be very easily bridged permanently, every material being ready on the spot. I ascertained from the Indians by inquiry that they were not subject to periodical sickness, and they communicated to me much interesting, and I believe reliable information regarding their numbers, manners and customs, and those of the other tribes of which they had any knowledge. The 15th and 16th were occupied in crossing the creeks, which was a matter of labor and difficulty to accomplish, and in conducting an examination of the country in their vicinity. On the 17th, bidding adieu to our

---

24. Telamni, according to Cook.
25. Ga'wia, from whom the name Kaweah derives.

friends, the Cowees, we started for King river; our course lay over
a barren and sandy plain, interspersed here and there with spots of
vegetation, but in general a perfect contrast to the rich soil upon the
river Frances. About six miles from the fifth creek we observed four
isolated hills, or buttes, about six hundred feet high, two of them
ranging nearly north and south, and about two miles apart; the other
two about three miles further to the east. At the first of these there
is a constant spring of water, and on the eastern side of the hill, about
three hundred yards from the spring, a deep circular excavation or
shaft, with the remains of an old windlass lying in its vicinity. We
were somewhat puzzled to account for this trace of human labor at
such a distance from any settlement; but I presume it to be the
remains of a well, dug many years ago by the Spanish soldiers of the
missions, who, we know, were accustomed to make excursions into
these plains for the laudable purpose of seizing upon and christianiz-
ing their wild inhabitants. We arrived upon the banks of King river
about five p.m., having travelled 23.66 miles in a direct line across
the plain. We found here two enterprising men, named Jones and
Rider, who with much difficulty had got a whale-boat up to this point,
and stretching a strong rope across the river, had established a ferry.
They informed us that there was another ferry about five miles
above them, kept by a man named Hampton, who, with another man
and themselves, formed the entire population of that part of the
country. We encamped at their ferry, and crossing the party upon the
18th, I took two or three men and rode up the northern bank about
fifteen miles to examine the river, and the character of the country in
its vicinity.

King river is the largest stream in the valley, at this time about
three hundred yards wide, with a rapid current and the water cold as
ice. It is about sixty miles in length, rising in two branches high up in
the Sierra, which, uniting about forty miles from its mouth, flow in a
southwest direction through the hills and valley, and empty into the
Taché lake at its northeast extremity. Its banks are high and well timbered, and the country in its immediate vicinity is apparently fertile.
It forms five sloughs like the Frances, but they are much wider, and
the country between them is swampy and difficult of access. There
are no less than seventeen rancherias of Indians upon this river, numbering in all, probably about three thousand, including those situated

among the hills in the vicinity. Of these, those living upon the lower part of the river are friendly and well disposed towards the whites; those high up among the hills are entirely ignorant, treacherous, and mischievous. I was informed by Colonel Hampton, at the upper ferry, that the Cho-e-minee rancheria,[26] situated in his vicinity, and numbering about ninety warriors, had been quite troublesome of late, using his horses without permission, and in one instance attempting to take his boat to ferry over a party of Sonorans. I thought his isolated position, surrounded by these mischievous savages, one of considerable danger, but he appeared to feel no apprehension of their committing any overt act of hostility.

On my return to the encampment I found a party of Indians, armed with bows and arrows, had passed down upon the southern bank, stopping at the ferryman's hut, and telling the occupants that they must leave that part of the country in four days. The ferrymen were not at all alarmed, however, and I think that our presence, and the knowledge that a body of troops were soon to be stationed in their neighborhood, had a very salutary restraining effect upon these Indians, who, I believe, would become exceedingly troublesome if they had no dread of the consequences. It was this band that murdered Garner and his companions in 1849.[27] We left the ferry on the 19th, and travelling south west for 19.84 miles encamped on the edge of a swamp at a point about three miles above the mouth of King river and immediately opposite the No-tanto village.[28] As this point had been indicated in my instructions for examination as a suitable site for a military post, I was anxious to cross the river and visit it, but was informed by the Indians, a large body of whom swam across to our encampment, that all the country in the vicinity was

---

26. The Choinimni, who occupied the foothills and the eastern edge of the valley.
27. William Robert Garner, born in London, England in 1803, and deserted from an English whaler in 1824 or 1826 at Santa Barbara. He had what can only be described as a checkered career. He was, variously, in the lumber business, a clerk, policeman, translator, auctioneer, and alcalde's secretary, and an explorer for gold—which led to his death. See page 16, where Carson has his name as Gardner.
28. See footnote 1, page 75. "Within a year or two after Derby's visit the village of Notonto was attacked by American cattlemen and farmers. The rancheria was devastated and 200 of the 300 people present were massacred in cold blood." (S. F. Cook.)

overflown, and that it would be impossible to cross, even if we were
to construct balsas of tulé, owing to the rapidity of the current. It
was evident enough that the country was overflown, and as I found it
impossible for anything but an Indian to get even to the bank of the
river, I was reluctantly obliged to give up any idea of crossing at this
point. I could see enough of the country, however, upon the other side
to satisfy myself that it would be a very unpleasant place for anything but Indians to occupy, and the fact of our not being able to get
at it at all would be a sufficient proof of its non-eligibility in a military point of view. The No-tantoes are the finest looking Indians I
have met with in the valley. All that came over to our encampment
were large well built athletic men, nearly six feet high, and their
physiognomy struck me as less repulsive than that of the Tachés and
other Indians whom we had seen. Their captain was an old Indian
named Antonio. He had certificates of recommendation from Colonel
Mason[29] and others, which, by his friendly appearance and offers of
assistance to the extent of his abilities, appeared to be well merited.
He stated the number of No-tantoes at about three hundred, and
informed us that he had never seen the waters so high as they had
risen this season. I ascertained from him that the months of August
and September are a very sickly period at this point; and was afterwards satisfied of this from information that I received from a respectable man who had crossed King river in the month of August at
the village, and who found its inhabitants prostrated by sickness to
such an extent that he could get no assistance from them in crossing.

On the 20th we marched 24.92 miles in a devious course with the
object of striking the "Sanjon de San Jose," which is a slough connecting the river San Joaquin with the Taché lake, but were unable to get
further on account of the mire, the ground between the lake and the
San Joaquin being entirely cut up by small sloughs which had overflown in every direction, making the country a perfect swamp, which
I found it a matter of great difficulty to cross. We saw numerous
bands of wild horses, numbering in all more than a thousand; they
were at some distance, but their appearance rendered me extremely

---

29. Richard Barnes Mason, the military governor of California from May 1847 to
February 1849.

anxious for the safety of my animals, which would infallibly have
been lost if they could have broken loose and joined them, as they
appeared much inclined to do. We were engaged on the 21st, 22d and
23d in getting through the mire, crossing no less than eight distinct
sloughs, one of which we were obliged to raft over, before arriving
at the Sanjon. In all of these sloughs a strong current was running
southwest, or from the San Joaquin river to the lake. The country
over which we passed between these sloughs was miserable in the
extreme, and our animals suffered terribly for want of grass. There
being no wood upon the plain except an occasional willow on the
largest slough we could make no fires, and were consequently
obliged to return to bread and water, a diet which, though simple in
the extreme, I somewhat preferred to the raw salt pork on which the
men luxuriated. The "Sanjon de San Jose" is a large and deep slough
about forty miles in length, connecting the waters of the Taché lake
with the San Joaquin river, with which it unites at its great southern
bend. At this time it was about two hundred and forty feet in width,
and with an extremely slow current setting towards the river. I do
not think it possible to communicate directly with the lake through
this slough. An attempt had been made a week or two previous to
our arrival by a party of men in a whale-boat, who examined it for
twenty or thirty miles, and found it branching off into innumerable
smaller sloughs, which intersected the Tulé swamp in every direction. They also reported that there was a fall of water about six or
eight feet at this point. I think it highly probable that there may be
a rapid near the mouth of the slough, but should find it difficult to
account for a direct fall of that height; and as I could hear of no one
else who had seen it, although I met with many who had crossed the
Sanjon in every direction during the dry season, I am inclined to disbelieve in its existence. The whole country for forty miles in extent
in a southerly direction by ten in width, between the San Joaquin
river and the Taché lake, is, during the rainy season and succeeding
months until the middle of July, a vast swamp everywhere intersected by sloughs, which are deep, miry and dangerous. A wagon
road therefore crossing the Sanjon at any point is impracticable, as
it could not by any possibility be travelled more than three months
in the year. I regret that we were unable to follow up the Sanjon to
the lake, but this was utterly impossible. We found that we could

not proceed a quarter of a mile in either direction without getting hopelessly mired, and as the water was fast rising, we could not get back over the swamp which we had already with great exertion and difficulty crossed. There was neither wood nor grass where we struck the slough, and though without any materials for building a raft, it became necessary to cross it immediately. In this emergency a man of my party volunteered to swim the Sanjon, and proceed on foot to the nearest ferry upon the river San Joaquin for the purpose of procuring a boat. This course was adopted and the boat brought up by a Mr. Bridger from the upper ferry at the southern bend of the river, arriving that evening. We succeeded in crossing the animals and arriving at the high land upon the bend early upon the 24th.

The river San Joaquin, rising in the spurs of the Sierra Nevada, flows in a southwest direction for about sixty miles to a point, where making a great bend of over 90° it changes its course to the north-west, emptying finally into Suisun bay. At the time of our arrival its waters were at their highest stage; the back water from the river had filled the innumerable sloughs extending from its banks in every direction across the valley. And I was informed by parties arriving at the ferry on their way to the mines, that the whole country to the north was overflown, and that large numbers of men and animals were encamping upon the plains, finding it impossible to proceed further by land and being unable to cross the river. The point upon which we were encamped at the southern bend, was about ten feet above the level of the stream, and for two miles in extent north and south was not overflown. A road from the debouche of the passes of Santa Anna and Pacheo [Pacheco], distant above twenty-five miles, might therefore, crossing here, be made available as a means of com-munication with the eastern side of the lake, and the streams flowing into it at any season of the year. At this time the river at this point was about two hundred yards wide and from ten to twenty feet in depth, but during the dry season it falls from four to two and a half feet. I think, however, that a large boat could ascend the river *to the bend* during nine months in the year; its further progress would be prevented at any time by the sand bar formed by the confluence of the Sanjon, which extends across the bed of the river and is covered by about two feet of water at its highest stages.

Misión San Carlos Borromeo de Carmelo—Carmel Mission. Drawing by Edward Vischer, 1861.

Finding it impossible to proceed further down the valley with
advantage, I started upon the 27th from the San Joaquin to the
south, skirting the western coast of the Taché lake on my return
march. I had previously sent two men to Monterey with orders to
proceed through the pass of Santa Anna, (of which no examination
has yet been made,) and to ascertain whether or not a wagon road
might be made through it.

At a distance of twenty-two miles from the San Joaquin, we
crossed the dry bed of a stream flowing during the rainy season from
the coast range to the lake, upon the banks of which are found a few
cottonwood trees and a little grass; but with this exception the whole
valley south of the bend between the coast range and the Taché lake
we found a miserable barren, sandy desert, with no vegetation but a
few straggling artemisias, and no inhabitants but a few attenuated
rabbits and gophers. We encamped upon a slough connecting with
the Sanjon upon the 28th, where I observed some singular ducks
of a light red or claret color, with a white bill and short black tail,
and others of brilliant black plumage with red bill and feet, resembling very much turkey-buzzards in their general appearance. I was
anxious to obtain some specimens of these birds, but although we
shot several we were unable to get them from the water. We encamped upon the shore of the lake upon the 29th, having made 17.32
miles and on the 30th reached the debouche of the pass of San Miguel
having travelled 24.60 miles, passing on our route the rancheria of
the Tinta Tachés, situated upon the northeast extremity of the lake
and containing about two hundred and fifty or three hundred inhabitants. A few of them visited our encampment, two of whom could
speak Spanish, and left well pleased with the treatment they received. We took up our line of march for Monterey by the same route
that we had pursued in coming out upon the 31st, and arrived there
without incident upon Saturday the 8th of June.

The Tularé valley, from the mouth of the Mariposa to the Tejon
pass at its head, is about one hundred and twenty miles in extent,
and varies from eight to one hundred miles in width. With the exception of a strip of fertile land upon the rivers emptying with the lakes
from the east, it is little better than a desert. The soil is generally
dry, decomposed and incapable of cultivation, and the vegetation,
consisting of artemisias and wild sage, is extremely sparse. The only

point in the whole valley which struck me as at all suitable for a military post was the small portion of interval land contained by the five creeks of the river Frances. A position here would be central, being easy of communication with King river to the north and with Kern river to the south, upon which two streams and their tributaries are situated the greater number of Indian rancherias in the valley. The land is excellent for cultivation, well timbered, and abundance of building material may be found in the vicinity, either stone or heavy pine and oak timber. A road leading through the Téjon pass from Los Angelos, and intersecting the emigrant trail through Walker's pass near Kern river, passes directly through this point to the northern mines of the San Joaquin valley. This road will undoubtedly be much travelled when brought into notice, and the post being established at this point, will contribute much to its safety and protection. The post could be supplied by wagons through the pass of San Miguel, either from San Luis Obispo or Monterey, or by a wagon road from Monterey through the pass of Pacheco or Santa Anna, crossing the San Joaquin at its southern bend, and King river at the lower ferry.

From the information regarding the character of the San Joaquin between Stockton and the southern bend, I have no doubt that it may be navigated by small steamboats to the latter points, during eight or nine months of the year. In this case, this would be by all means the most desirable route of communication, as a depot might be established upon the high land at the southern bend, which would be but two short days' journey from the post. I should judge that the lake, from the difficulty of getting to its shores, and the swamps and sloughs that everywhere environ it, could never be made available as a means of communication, though, if this were possible, a ferry upon its waters would shorten the distance to its east bank by over fifty miles. The whole number of Indians in the valley, as near as I can judge, is about four thousand. These are by no means connected with each other; the Rancherias upon the southern rivers being in fact ignorant of the existence of those situated further to the north. Those who have had an opportunity of becoming acquainted with the whites, are friendly and well-disposed; the others, although ignorant, mischievous and perhaps maliciously inclined, may easily be kept in subjection by a small force, and by kind treatment. I have the honor to enclose a map and copy of the valley, showing the various routes, and the geographical position of the various points referred to in this report; also two tables, one of latitudes and longitudes, the other of distances, as measured by the viameter.

I am, sir, with high respect, your obedient servant,

GEO. H. DERBY,
Brevet First Lieutenant Topographical Engineers.

Major E. R. S. CANBY,
Adjutant General tenth military department.

Table of Geographical positions on the route pursued by Lieutenant G. H. Derby, in the reconnaissance of the Tulare plains, April and May, 1850.

Places of observation.	North latitude.	Longitude west of Greenwich
San Miguel	35° 38′ 00″	120° 27′ 00″
Santa Margarita	35° 18′ 22″	120° 11′ 00″
Estrella	35° 36′ 00″	120° 13′ 00″
Moore's Creek	35° 46′ 43″	
Gopher Creek	35° 40′ 30″	
Cottonwood Creek	35° 26′ 41″	
Kern River	35° 18′ 00″	
West point of Buena Vista Lake . .	35° 08′ 23″	
Tulé River	35° 50′ 30″	119° 07′ 00″
Frances River	36° 15′ 50″	119° 14′ 00″
King River (Jones's Ferry)	36° 24′ 47″	119° 28′ 00″
Sanjon de San Jose		120° 04′ 00″
West point of Taché Lake	36° 48′ 00″	119° 49′ 18″

Editor's note: It should not be surprising that Lt. Derby's latitudes and longitudes do not agree with those that have been achieved with modern methods. Only the first three locales in the above list are precise places, since it is not possible to know just where Derby crossed a particular creek or reached the shore of a particular lake. As an example, the correct contemporary coordinates for San Miguel are latitude 35° 45′ 09″, longitude 120° 41′ 43″, a kind and degree of error that is true of all the entries. Derby's figures are too far south and too far east—but by very small amounts.

Table of distances on the route pursued by Lieutenant G. H. Derby, in the reconnaissance of the Tulare plain, April and May, 1850.

	Miles.	Miles.
From Monterey to the Toros Ranch		12.00
Rancho de Guadaloupe	9.00	21.00
Rancho de Buena Vista	8.00	29.00
Soledad	12.80	41.80
Camp near San Benitia	25.81	67.61
Camp near Ojitas	26.25	93.86
San Miguel	29.61	123.47
Santa Margarita	31.25	154.72
San Louis Obispo	10.00	164.72
From San Miguel to Estrella	12.75	136.22
Dick's creek encampment	29.51	165.73
Outlet of Ton Taché Lake	30.04	195.77
Moore's Creek (upper camp)	34.46	230.23
Cottonwood Creek	24.27	264.50
Kern River	12.00	276.50
North point of Buena Vista Lake	16.80	293.30
From Moore's Creek to Tulé River	7.16	237.39
Frances River (west side of slough)	24.93	262.32
King River (Jones' Ferry)	23.26	285.58

Index

Cover design by Larry Van Dyke and Peter Browning
Text typeface: Century Expanded 10/13
Printed on 60-lb. Glatfelter Natural, B-16, acid-free
Printing and binding by McNaughton & Gunn, Inc., Saline, Michigan

You can order additional copies of this book directly from the publisher. Price: — $12.95

Also available from Great West Books:
In the Heart of the Sierras: Yo Semite Valley and the Big Tree Groves, by James M. Hutchings. Republished for the first time since the 1880s. The story of the Mariposa Indian War of 1851, and the discovery of Yosemite Valley; the first tourists to Yosemite; the Calaveras Big Trees; routes of travel from San Francisco to Yosemite; lives of the Indians; the scenic wonders of Yosemite and its High Sierra. 592 pages, 6 x 9, 192 illustrations, historic map, index. Hard cover: **$44.95.** Paperback: **$29.95.**

The Last Wilderness: 600 miles by canoe and portage in the Northwest Territories, by Peter Browning. Two men travel from northern Saskatchewan to Great Slave Lake, seeing no other people for 74 days. Paperback, 192 pages, 7 x 10, two maps, 59 photos, 60 other illustrations, extensive northern bibliography. **$14.95.**

Tahoe Place Names: The origin and history of names in the Lake Tahoe Basin, by Barbara Lekisch. Historic photos of early maps; old names and Indian names; diary of Charles Preuss from January–February 1844. Paperback, 192 pages, 6 x 9, 39 photos, bibliography. **$11.95.**

Yosemite Place Names: The History of Geographic Names in Yosemite National Park, by Peter Browning. Old names, Indian names, and early newspaper stories, including the account of the first tourist group to visit Yosemite Valley, in 1855. Paperback, 256 pages, 6 x 9, reference map, 27 photos, bibliography. **$12.95.**

John Muir, In His Own Words: A Book of quotations, compiled and edited by Peter Browning. The best of John Muir—the essence of his thought and beliefs. **"Earth has no sorrow that earth cannot heal."** Paperback, 112 pages, 6 x 9, extensive index. **$9.95.**

Place Names of the Sierra Nevada: From Abbot to Zumwalt, by Peter Browning. Covers the area from Walker Pass to the northern boundary of Alpine County. 264 Pages, 6 x 9, 15 photos, bibliography. Paperback, second edition 1991: **$12.95.** Hard cover, with addenda: **$19.95.**

Order form on next page

To order

- Please enclose payment with your order. We accept checks and money orders, payable in U.S. funds.
- If your order is being shipped to a California address, please add **8.25%** sales tax.
- **Postage and handling charges are:**
  $2.00 for one book, and 50¢ for each additional book.

Discounts

- Orders over $50: 10% discount, and free shipping.
- Orders over $100: 20% discount, and free shipping.

Order Form

Mail to: Great West Books • P.O. Box 1028 • Lafayette, CA 94549 • (510) 283-3184

____ **Bright Gem of the Western Seas** @ $12.95 _____

____ **In the Heart of the Sierras** (hard) @ $44.95_____

____ **In the Heart of the Sierras** (paper) @ 29.95_____

____ **The Last Wilderness** @ $14.95 _____

____ **Tahoe Place Names** @ $11.95 _____

____ **Yosemite Place Names** @ $12.95 _____

____ **John Muir, In His Own Words** @ $9.95 _____

Subtotal: _____

Discount, if applicable: _____

Subtotal: _____

CA addresses add **8.25%** sales tax: _____

Postage & handling: _____

Total enclosed: _____

Name _____

Address _____

(Please _____

Print) _____